EDUCATION RESOURCE CENTER
UNIVERSITY OF DELAWARE

Classroom Critters

and the Scientific Method

Sally Kneidel

T 35394

991822

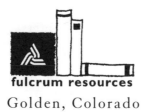

fulcrum resources

Golden, Colorado

Sci
K 734
1999

Copyright © 1999 Sally Kneidel

All rights reserved.

No part of this book may be reproduced, stored in a retrieval system, or transmitted in any form or by any means, electronic, mechanical, photocopying, recording, or otherwise, without the prior written permission of the publisher.

Library of Congress Cataloging-in-Publication Data
  Kneidel, Sally Stenhouse.
    Classroom critters and the scientific method / Sally Kneidel.
      p.   cm.
    ISBN 1-55591-969-3 (pbk.)
      1. Animals—Study and teaching (Elementary). 2. Animals—
  Experiments. 3. Animal behavior—Experiments. I. Title.
  QL51.K54   1999
    372.3'57—DC21   98-49128
                                                    CIP

Printed in the United States of America
0 9 8 7 6 5 4 3 2

Book design: Linda Mae Tratechaud, LiMiTeD Edition Book Design
Interior photographs: Sally Kneidel
Cover illustration copyright © 1999 Petica Berry

The textface of this book was set in Granjon 11/14,
and the display was set in Futura.

Fulcrum Publishing
350 Indiana Street, Suite 350
Golden, Colorado 80401-5093
(800) 992-2908 • (303) 277-1623
www.fulcrum-resources.com

*To all the fine students
at Cotswold Elementary,
Bain Elementary,
and Dilworth Elementary
who have enriched my life.*

Table of Contents

Acknowledgments ix

Introduction xi

CHAPTER 1: HAMSTERS, GERBILS, AND PET MICE

Experiment 1. Are Mice Wall-Seekers? 1

Experiment 2. Do Mice Prefer Tunnels of a Particular Diameter? 6

Experiment 3. Do Mice Prefer Tunnels (Tubes) Open on One End or Two? 11

Experiment 4. How Fast Can a Rodent Learn to Make the "Correct" Turn Consistently, to Find a Food Treat, in a T-Maze? 16

Experiment 5. Will a Mouse Consistently Alternate Directions in a Forced-Turn Maze? 22

Experiment 6. How Does a Food Reward Affect a Mouse's Performance in a Complex Maze? 27

Experiment 7. Which Is Faster—Hamster, Gerbil, or Mouse? 32

Experiment 8. Do Gerbils Seek the Company of Other Gerbils? 37

Experiment 9. Are Male Mice and Female Mice Equally Aggressive Toward Male "Intruders"? 43

Experiment 10. Does Aggression in a Male Mouse Depend Upon the Sex of the Intruder? 48

Experiment 11. Is a Male Gerbil More Aggressive Toward an Intruder That Is Familiar or One That Is Not Familiar? 53

Experiment 12. Which Is More Aggressive—a Resident or an Intruder? **57**

Experiment 13. Are Gerbils Territorial? That Is, Do Adult Gerbils Living Together Use Different Portions of the Terrarium? **59**

Experiment 14. Can We Predict, on the Basis of Past Behavior, Which Gerbil Will Back Away from a Confrontation in a Tunnel and Which One Won't? **64**

Experiment 15. Which Scents Cause a Reaction in a Hamster? **69**

Experiment 16. Does the Scent of a Cat in a Terrarium Affect the Amount of Exploratory Behavior Displayed by a Gerbil? **73**

Experiment 17. At What Age Do Mice Develop a Sensitivity to Odors? Which Odors Are They Sensitive To? **78**

Experiment 18. At What Age Do Mice Develop the Ability to Right Themselves When Flipped Over? **84**

Experiment 19. Does Mouse Development Follow the Same Sequence of Stages (Moving Limbs, Lifting Head, Creeping on Belly, Crawling on All Fours) That Human Development Does? **87**

Experiment 20. When Does the Ability to Rope-Climb Develop in Mice? **91**

CHAPTER 2: GOLDFISH AND GUPPIES

Experiment 21. Do Goldfish Hide? **94**

Experiment 22. What Is the Effect of Chilling on the Breathing Rate of Goldfish? **98**

Experiment 23. What Is the Effect of Chilling on the Rate of Movement of Goldfish? **102**

Experiment 24. Do Goldfish Eat Fewer Guppies When There Is Elodea Throughout the Aquarium? **105**

Experiment 25. Are Guppies More Attracted to Hiding Places When Predators Are Present? **108**

Experiment 26. Do Fish Seek Out the Company of Other Fish? **112**

Experiment 27. Can a Goldfish Be Trained to Come to Your Hand for Food? **116**

Experiment 28. Can a Goldfish Be Trained to Touch a Black Circle in Response to a Hand Signal? **119**

CHAPTER 3: ANOLIS LIZARDS (ANOLES)

Experiment 29.   Do Anoles Prefer Mealworms or Crickets?   122

Experiment 30.   How Do Male Anoles Respond to Their Own Image in a Mirror?   126

Experiment 31.   Will a Male Anole Respond to a Photograph of Another Male, or Does the Image Have to Be Moving?   129

Experiment 32.   Will an Anole Change Color in Response to a Color Change in Its Surroundings?   132

CHAPTER 4: KITTENS AND PUPPIES

Experiment 33.   Do Kittens Prefer Human Contact More Than Cats Do?   137

Experiment 34.   Which Chooses Human Contact More—a Kitten or a Puppy?   143

Experiment 35.   Is a Heated Stuffed Animal More Attractive to a Kitten for Company Than a Cool Stuffed Animal?   148

Experiment 36.   Will a Kitten Choose Another Kitten for Company?   152

Experiment 37.   Do Kittens Show Left- or Right-Handedness?   155

Notes   160

Index of Experiments   161

Acknowledgments

I wish to thank the students at Cotswold Elementary, as well as family and friends, who carried out the experiments and allowed themselves to be photographed.

Thanks especially to Margaret Rowe, Micki Tucker, and Heather Sutherland, Cotswold teachers whose cooperation and assistance were invaluable.

I would also like to thank Lavender-N-Lace Pet Shoppe, especially Carol W. Scott, for years of friendly help and advice with rodents, fish, kittens, and puppies.

Introduction

Whom Is the Book For?

This is a book for teachers, parents, and students.

For teachers: this book will help you kill two birds with one stone. The experiments described here will teach your students a lot of science content—animal behavior, ecology, and vertebrate characteristics. But perhaps more important, with the shifting emphasis in science curricula and state science tests, these experiments will teach your students science process skills.

Teaching science today is more and more about teaching students experimentation—making hypotheses and gathering data to test the hypotheses. Each experiment in the book uses all the steps of the scientific method. Your students will become familiar with the steps, as well as with some of the more elusive principles inherent in the scientific method. What is a control, and why is it necessary? What is an experimental variable, and why must an experiment have only one? Why does an experiment need more than one trial?

The experiments in the book not only will help students master what they need to know in the classroom, but also will help prepare them for science fairs.

For parents and students: this is a science project resource book. Not only does it explain every aspect of the scientific method required by science fairs, but it suggests thirty-seven topics. Most can be done in less than an hour. And most require only commonly available household materials. Pet store animals are inexpensive, many less than a dollar. Some pet stores will lend animals for science projects, and most will accept returns of purchased hamsters, gerbils, mice, fish, etc., if you want the animals only temporarily.

The Format of the Book

The description of each experiment tells you the scientific steps involved—the question, hypothesis, materials, methods, results, and conclusion. Each description also identifies the experimental variable, the control, the dependent variable, and the controlled variables, and tells you how to do multiple trials. (Worksheets are provided for every experiment.) After you have done a few experiments in the book, you will be able to extrapolate the process and apply it to other questions that students may bring up, or questions suggested by your classwork.

There are several experiments in the book that specify a test-animal of a particular sex. In these experiments, I have used male or female pronouns accordingly.

For most of the experiments, the sex of the animal is irrelevant. In many of these experiments, I refer to the animal as "it." However, in some of them, I have referred to the animal as "he" even though you may use a female. No offense is intended. I have done this because the pronoun "it" must be used to refer to the various objects in the experiment. Using a gender pronoun to indicate the animal simply helps me to avoid the confusing overuse of "it."

I could have randomly alternated the use of "he" and "she" instead of "it." In a book of this nature, I think that solution has problems also. It creates confusion about which gender changes are random, and which are intentional and necessary.

The Principles of the Scientific Method

A situation where observations are made and recorded does not in itself constitute an experiment. If I notice that cardinals don't use the bird feeder outside my window, but they frequently use the feeder in my neighbor's tree, that's just an observation. It's not an experiment because it tells me nothing about cause and effect, nothing about why she has cardinals and I don't. It could be the location, or the type of seeds, or maybe the type of feeder.

An unexplained observation often becomes the starting point for an experiment by arousing curiosity. Now I have a question. I follow this with a prediction, my hypothesis, which I then test with an experiment. For example, I might guess that my neighbor has cardinals and I don't because of the difference in location. To test my hypothesis, I need to change the location of my feeder but leave everything else the same. If my cardinal count is consistently much higher when my feeder is in a tree than it is when the feeder is outside the window (my results), then I have shown experimentally that the location of the feeder makes a difference to the cardinals.

Experimental Variable

The one aspect I decide to change, or vary, is the experimental variable. In the above experiment, with the feeder located by the window and then moved to the tree, the experimental variable is location. All other aspects that could possibly influence the birds, such as seed type and feeder type, season and time of day, and nearby human activity, are kept the same. They are controlled variables. I am controlling any effect they may have by keeping them the same.

One way to identify an experimental variable is to ask, "I'm looking at the effect of *what?*" If I'm looking at the effect of feeder location on cardinals, then feeder location is my experimental variable.

The reason for having only one experimental variable is obvious in this situation. If I also vary the seed type, then are the differences I notice in the number of cardinals due to different seed types or different locations? It would be impossible to say.

The Control

The control just gives you something to compare your results with. In the bird feeder example, the feeder is moved to a new location in a tree in the middle of the yard. We're looking at the effect of a new location on the number of cardinals using the feeder. The control here would be the cardinal count at the old location by the window. The only difference between the two sets of observations is location. If we didn't have any observations recorded from the old location (the control), then it would be impossible to say anything about the effect of the new location.

Multiple Trials or Replicates

If a student wanted to be confident that the difference between the two locations was real, then it would be a good idea to repeat the counts several times. Five periods of observation at each location would probably be adequate, each period lasting about 15 minutes. The student would count the number of cardinals observed at the feeder during each observation period, average the five counts near the house, average the five counts away from the house, and compare the two averages.

Three trials are adequate for many experiments when the results are consistent. The more variation there is among the experimental trials, the more trials you need to be confident of your conclusions. Birds come to feeders sporadically, so there probably would be a lot of variation among trials in an experiment like this.

Data Collecting

Data collected in the form of counts or measurements are preferable to subjective comparisons such as "The fish in the cooler water moved more slowly than those in the warmer water." Numbers give a means of clear, objective comparison. They're less subject to experimenter bias or self-fulfilling expectations, and more accurately communicate the results to other people. Numbers can be graphed, and graphs, more than any number of words, can summarize quickly the relationship between cause and effect. One glance at a graph will tell you the relationship between the number of jumping jacks and the number of heartbeats per minute, or the relationship between the aquarium water temperature and the number of grid lines the fish crossed per minute (a measure of the fish's rate of movement).

Using numbers is important too because science is often simply about quantifying ordinarily observed phenomena. For example, you might suspect intuitively that people tend to feel more gloomy on overcast days than on sunny days. But if someone is able to demonstrate this numerically, with a mood index and a light-intensity measure, that's science. Such an experiment might be useful in planning interior lighting in a work facility.

The Steps for Reporting Your Experiment

Question

The question asks what the effect is of ... whatever variable interests you. What is the effect of location on birds' use of a feeder? What is the effect of temperature on fish's rate of movement? The question doesn't have to be worded that way, but in most experiments it can be. Asking "What is the effect of ... ?" can help you identify your experimental variable.

Hypothesis

If your experiment is based on an observation of something like the two feeders, then your hypothesis is a statement of what you think is causing the observed difference between the two. More often, though, experiments start from a single observation. You observe that rodents like to run through cardboard tubes, so you wonder if they have a preference for a particular tube diameter. Your hypothesis here would be just your prediction of which tube diameter they prefer.

Materials

The materials section is simply a listing of all the materials used in the experiment, and is specific enough that a reader could duplicate your materials closely.

Methods or Procedure

Experiments published in scientific journals generally have a combined "Materials and Methods" section where the materials, and what was done with them, are described at the same time. But science fairs usually require a separate listing of materials.

In the methods or procedure section, the experimenter describes what was done to set up and carry out the experiment, in such a way that a reader could repeat the experiment almost exactly.

Results

Here the experimenter simply reports what happened. Ideally, the results include counts or measurements. How many cardinals came to the feeder each day when it hung in the tree? How many came when the feeder was next to the house? Any other pertinent information can be given here. For example, "Cardinals came only in the morning"; or, "Cats were observed around the feeder site next to the house." Science students sooner or later will need to learn to present data both in table form and graphically.

Conclusion

In this section the experimenter either accepts or rejects the hypothesis, giving an answer to the original question: "My hypothesis was right. More cardinals came to the feeder when it was in the tree." In the conclusion, the experimenter also attempts to explain the results: "Originally I thought the cardinals might be afraid of human activity near the house. But now I wonder if they are afraid of the cats." Any other remarks that would be considered further discussion of the results should go in the conclusion.

Graphing

On a graph, the experimental variable generally goes on the horizontal axis. The experimental variable is also called the independent variable. The variable that changed because of the experimental variable is called the dependent variable and goes on the vertical axis.

For example, if you tested the effect of temperature on fish's breathing rates at several different temperatures,

Alexis holds a mouse for the first time.

then temperature would go along the horizontal axis. The fish's breathing rate depends upon the temperature; so as the dependent variable, the breathing rate would go on the vertical axis. Or you could say that the fish's breathing rate changes because of the temperature. Obviously the water temperature doesn't change because of the fish's breathing rate.

Many of the experiments in this book will be comparing counts in two categories, a situation that doesn't lend itself to line graphs but can be represented with a bar graph or histogram. One example is the "Do goldfish hide?" experiment. The two categories are the shaded half of the fish container and the unshaded half. The presence or absence of shading is the experimental or independent variable, so the histogram labels "in the shade" and "in the open" go on the horizontal axis. The number of fish on each end depends upon the shading, so the number of fish is the dependent variable and goes along the vertical axis.

For most experiments, one or more completed graphs are shown, as an example of how you could graph one possible outcome. They are just examples. Also provided are one or more blank graphs for you to copy and fill in with your own data.

About Using Mice

Many adults think they don't like mice, and you may be one of them. Just a quick word in defense of mice before you dismiss them. Every time I pass a class in the hall, several students step out of line to ask me hopefully, "Are we gonna use the mice this week in lab?" When they walk into my room and see a mouse experiment set out, the response is a collective, emphatic "Yessssss!" I don't know why they like mice so much. I suspect part of it is that they believe their parents don't (although mice are the favorite at our Parents' Science Fair Workshop).

Students' interest in mice, though, goes beyond any unfair notoriety mice may have. The students find the mice appealing. A little white mouse has a lot of the same charms as a kitten or puppy. It washes its hands and face carefully like a kitten. It explores every nook and cranny of the cage like a puppy. The pink ears and pink nose make the animal look like a cartoon character. And part of the appeal must be the novelty. The students have all seen hamsters and gerbils, but few have gotten a close look at a mouse.

Hamsters and gerbils can be used in many of the rodent labs just as well, although gerbils are a bit slow at mazes. I prefer mice mainly because the students prefer them. But I would use them anyway. They're smaller and take up less space, they're easier to borrow at no cost from a pet store, and they're much cheaper if purchased. At the time of this writing, a mouse at the closest pet store was $1; a gerbil or hamster was $7. For me an important point is that they're easier to handle than hamsters and gerbils. You can easily lift mice by the tails, they weigh so little. Hamsters have no tails and some bite. Some gerbils bite, too. I've never been bitten

by a mouse. Also the mice are more active than hamsters, and the experiment may go faster.

Mice from pet stores are as tame as hamsters or gerbils, or more so. They do not carry diseases. Mice do eliminate waste, both kinds, more often than hamsters or gerbils, and so require more frequent newspaper or litter changes, but for me their small size, low price, ease of handling, popularity with students, and active nature, outweigh this one disadvantage.

Rodents Aren't All the Same

Mice, gerbils, and hamsters behave differently and will produce different results. Check the Materials sections carefully when planning experiments in Chapter 1. If it lists all three rodents (mouse, gerbil, hamster), then you can use any of the three. If it lists only one, then there is a reason for that. For example, mice tend to do mazes somewhat better than gerbils or hamsters, in my experience. So I've suggested mice for Experiment 6 involving a complex maze. Experiments 8 through 12 involve companionship and aggression. Mice, gerbils, and hamsters have very different social lives and will give different results. A single male mouse often lives with several adult females and their babies. When the male babies grow up, the adult male will expect them to leave. Adult male mice will not tolerate each other. Hamsters are solitary. Adults of either sex will fight, even if they are littermates. Adult gerbils can live peacefully with their own littermates, male or female, or with a mate. But adult gerbils that are strangers to one another will fight. You would not want to reveal all of this information to your students before doing Experiments 8 through 12, but it will help you in your planning.

CHAPTER 1

Hamsters, Gerbils, and Pet Mice

Question
Are Mice Wall-Seekers?

Hypothesis
I think mice will be against the wall in all / most / half / a few / no observations.

Materials
- at least one terrarium with a lid, or at least one cardboard box, 14 inches by 20 inches (35 cm x 50 cm) or larger, and 15 inches (38 cm) deep to keep the animal from jumping out
- one piece of blank paper cut to fit the inside floor of the terrarium or box exactly (newsprint or construction paper will work)
- one ruler or meter stick
- one black marker
- one mouse, hamster, or gerbil per terrarium or box
- one clock with a second hand

Procedure
To prepare each box or terrarium, cut a blank piece of paper to fit the inside of the box or terrarium exactly. With a black marker, draw a rectangle on the paper that is 2.5 inches (5 cm) from the outer edge at all points, to create a 2.5-inch (5 cm) pathway around the outermost part of the paper. Put the paper back into the terrarium or box. The

Alan's mouse interrupts its wall-seeking with an unsuccessful leap for freedom.

pathway is now against the wall, all the way around.

If you're doing this experiment with a large group and have only one mouse, you'll need a terrarium instead of a box so that everyone can see. If you have a large group and several mice, children can work in smaller groups with either cardboard boxes or terraria. Each group will need one mouse, one box with a pathway inside, one person to watch the clock, and at least one person to record data. To begin, the mouse is deposited in the box, by the tail, and one child immediately begins watching the clock and announces 10-second intervals. Another child records the location of the mouse every 10 seconds, for 2 minutes (twelve observations). After 2 minutes of this, the children can change roles and record for 2 more minutes. After this, they copy one another's data so that among them they have twenty-four observations—one for every 10 seconds for 4 minutes.

If you have only one animal and you decide to have the children work in small groups in sequence, the animal should be removed to its home between trials. Becoming habituated to the terrarium or box would probably affect its wall-seeking tendencies.

Adding trials in this experiment adds confidence that the results do reflect a real tendency in the animal, and are not just a consequence of the animal's being frightened by some particular noise, or being hungry or sleepy, or some other singular circumstance.

Results

Mice have a strong tendency to stay against the wall in a new container, and other rodents probably do as well. In many trials, all twenty-four

Alan's mouse stays against the wall.

tallies will be "Next to wall." In writing up the experiment, the children simply state the number of observations made in each of the two categories, "Next to wall" and "Away from wall," for the "Results" section of their report. They also can state any relevant observations, such as, "The mice walked in circles around the edge of the paper, standing up every few seconds to sniff the wall."

Conclusion

In the conclusion of an experiment, either verbally or in writing, the children either accept or reject their hypothesis, thereby answering the original question. This is the place too where they make sense of the observations recorded in the "Results." An attempt is made to explain the results and discuss their relevance to the animal's life or, possibly, human life. Most animals in strange situations move to a wall because it provides cover or protection on at least one side. Many of the children suggest that the mice or hamsters do it because they're looking for an escape route, and that may be right, too.

Identifying the Experimental Concepts

The **experimental variable** in this experiment is the wall. We are looking at the effect of the wall on the animal's choice of location.

The **control** here is having accessible space that is not against the wall, but is in other respects the same as the space against the wall. In this case, we keep the central area in the terrarium and the area along the wall the same by having the box or terrarium empty, with the paper blank.

The **dependent variable** is the mouse's location—the number of observations in each place (next to and away from the wall).

The **controlled variables** are all the things that could influence the animal's location in the container—food, water, litter, other animals—but are kept the same in all areas so they will not influence the results. Here, we've kept them the same by removing them entirely.

The need for **multiple trials** is met here by having several containers and several animals, or by having different groups of children carry out the procedure, or, if there are only one or two experimenters, by conducting at least three 2-minute trials.

Extension

The students may want to test how familiarity with the container affects wall-seeking behavior. After they have carried out the experiment as above, students can allow the animal time to get used to the terrarium or box and then repeat the experiment. If the animal is left in the enclosure for more than an hour, it will need food and water while it waits.

The experimental variable in this extension would be the degree of familiarity with the enclosure. You could test the effect of familiarity at different levels (after five minutes, one hour, one day in the terrarium, and so on). The control would be the data collected when the container was unfamiliar, the original data.

Encourage the children to think of other experimental variables that could affect wall-seeking, such as the presence of other animals, the presence of a refuge or a hiding place, and the presence of food or litter. Have them design experiments in writing to test their ideas, and say why they think these variables might affect the mouse's or hamster's behavior.

Extension

Do humans exhibit wall-seeking behavior? Have students record on family outings which tables are selected by the first few patrons in an almost empty restaurant. Are they along the wall or in the center? You'll need to control for the possible effect of differences in comfort by observing in restaurants that don't have booths along the wall. Here again, the experimental variable is the wall and the control is the central area of the room. Humans are indeed "wall-seekers"! I think we too feel safer (or more secure, or more comfortable) against a wall in a strange situation, perhaps unconsciously.

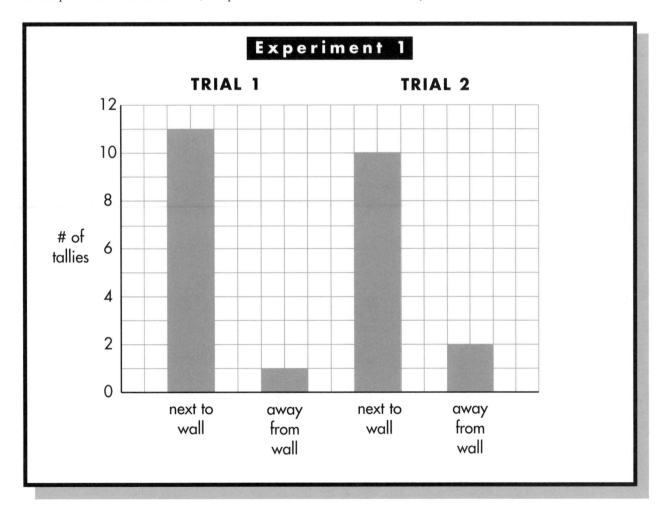

Experiment 1—A sample of how the data might turn out for one pair of students, one mouse. In each trial, a tally is made every 10 seconds for 2 minutes.

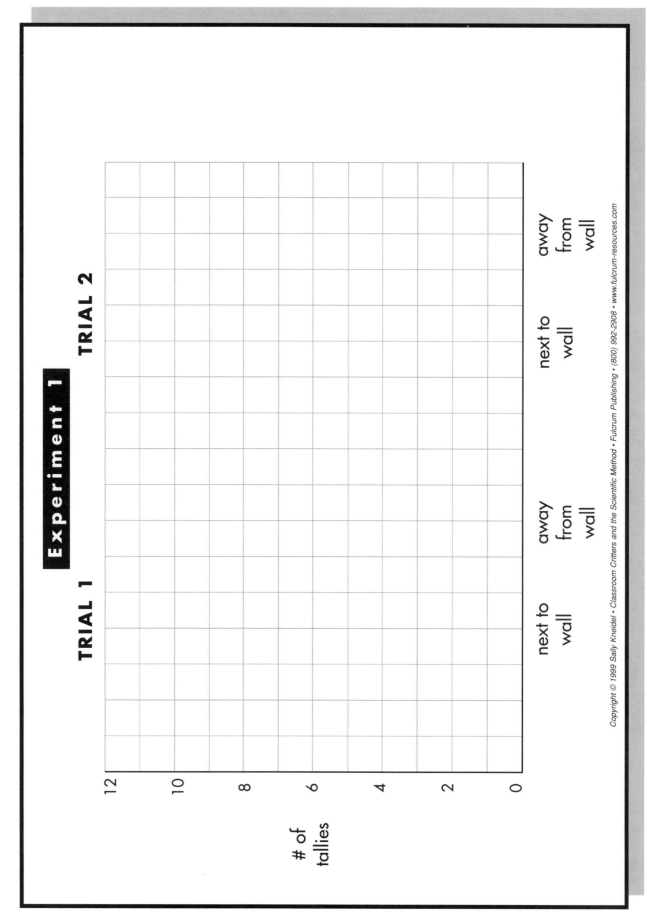

Experiment 1

TRIAL 1 **TRIAL 2**

next to wall | away from wall | next to wall | away from wall

# of tallies

12
10
8
6
4
2
0

Copyright © 1999 Sally Kneidel • Classroom Critters and the Scientific Method • Fulcrum Publishing • (800) 992-2908 • www.fulcrum-resources.com

Name: _____

Experiment 1

Question: Are mice wall-seekers?

Hypothesis: I think _____

_____

_____

Materials: _____ _____

_____ _____

Procedure: A black line was drawn 2.5 inches (5 cm) from the edge of the paper. The paper was fitted into the box. The mouse was placed in the center of the paper. In each trial, we tallied the mouse's position every 10 seconds for 2 minutes. We carried out _____ trials.

Results: (record tally marks in appropriate categories)

Next to wall	Away from wall

Total _____   Class total _____ | Total _____   Class total _____

Conclusion: _____

_____

_____

_____

_____

_____

Copyright © 1999 Sally Kneidel • Classroom Critters and the Scientific Method • Fulcrum Publishing • (800) 992-2908 • www.fulcrum-resources.com

Experiment 2

Question

Do Mice Prefer Tunnels of a Particular Diameter?

Hypothesis

I think mice prefer tunnels with a diameter of (a) 3 inches, (b) 2.5 inches, (c) 2 inches, or (d) 1.5 inches.

Materials

- at least one terrarium with a lid
- one hamster or mouse or gerbil
- four small sheets of construction paper of one color (a darker color will conceal stains better)
- clear tape

Procedure

The above materials are necessary for each experimental animal. If you have several animals and several terraria for several groups of children, each mouse will need a set of four tunnels. To make the tunnels, cut the construction paper into four pieces, measuring about 7 inches (18 cm) by 11 inches (28 cm). Each tunnel is going to be 7 inches (18 cm) long when completed. Roll up the four pieces of construction paper to make tunnels of these diameters:

- 3 inches (7.6 cm)
- 2.5 inches (6.4 cm)
- 2 inches (5 cm)
- 1.5 inches (3.8 cm).

These tunnel diameters work for mice. You may make them a little larger for hamsters or gerbils if they can't get through the smallest one or two tunnels.

You can probably collect enough data in trials of 10-minute durations. If you have one animal, do at least three 10-minute trials. If you have several animals, do one 10-minute trial per animal.

Decide in advance whether the children will tally a partial trip (entering and leaving through

Alan, Devon, and Andrew tally the mouse's choices.

Experiment 2

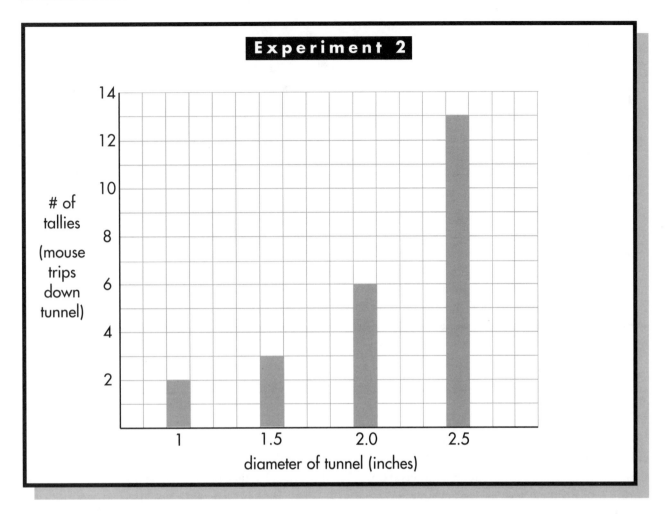

Experiment 2—The number of trips made by a single mouse over a period of 10 minutes. (The diameters in this graph are 1/2 inch smaller than those recommended. The recommended range is 1.5 inches to 3 inches.)

the same opening). Usually, the animals go all the way through the tunnel rather than turn around. But not always.

Results

The results depend on the size of your animal, with most animals preferring the 2.5- to 3-inch tunnels. The animals will have a definite preference for one diameter. If all your animals are roughly the same size, they'll probably all prefer the same tunnel diameter.

For the "Results" section of a write-up, the children state the number of tally marks for each tunnel diameter. "Results" also includes any relevant observations, such as, "Our animal was so big it couldn't fit in the smallest tunnel."

Conclusion

In this section, the children either accept or reject their own hypotheses. They also attempt to

explain the results. The explanations are often guesses, hopefully well-thought-out guesses.

My guess is that rodents prefer tunnels that are roughly the same size as the underground tunnels they might make in nature. The tunnel must be big enough to allow easy travel for the rodent, but small enough to exclude as many predators as possible. A lot of predators are skinny—weasels and snakes to name a couple.

Identifying the Experimental Concepts

The **experimental variable** in this experiment is the diameter of the tunnels. We're testing the effect of the diameter of the rodent's tunnel on its behavior.

The **control** here is the variety of diameters offered. If the animal prefers the 2.5-inch tunnel, we know that he does because we also offered 3-inch, 2-inch, and 1.5 inch tunnels. We know that the diameter alone affected his choice because we controlled all other aspects that could have affected his choice.

The **dependent variable** in this experiment is the rodent's reaction to the tunnel diameter, the variation in the number of trips down the four tunnels. His reaction depends on the diameter of the tunnels.

The **controlled variables** are all the factors that could influence the animal's choice. Tunnel color, tunnel texture, tunnel length, and tunnel placement could all affect the appeal of particular tunnels. So all these factors are not allowed to vary. Everything other than the tunnel diameter is held constant for all tunnels.

The need for **multiple trials** can be addressed here by having several groups of children conduct the test simultaneously with different animals. Or, if only one animal is available, the children can carry out three separate trials with that one.

Extension

The tunnel diameter experiment described above begins with the assumption that rodents will freely enter tunnels placed in their cages. Children may want to precede that experiment with a test of the underlying assumption. Will a rodent enter a tunnel in its cage? What would the experimental variable be?

Extension

Tunnels can vary in other aspects besides diameter. The children can offer tunnels of different lengths, or tunnels of different shades (black and white), or tunnels of different textures. In these three experiments, the experimental variable would be tunnel length, tunnel color, or tunnel texture, respectively.

Extension

Children also could offer transparent tunnels versus opaque tunnels. A clear tunnel can be made with an overhead transparency sheet. The opaque tunnel can be made by rolling up a transparency sheet and a piece of construction paper together, so the plastic is on the inside. This will control for texture—both clear and opaque tunnels will feel slick to the rodent's feet. The experimental variable is tunnel opacity. Of course, the tunnels' diameters will remain constant.

A different approach to tunnel-related behavior is to ask how bright light (a flashlight), thumping on the desk, or some other mild disturbance, affects the amount of time a rodent spends inside a tunnel.

The experimental variable here would be the presence or absence of a disturbance. Children can measure the amount of time spent in the tunnel by tallying the rodent's position (in or out) every 30 seconds, with or without a disturbance. These trials of 5 minutes each should produce enough data to see a difference, if there is one.

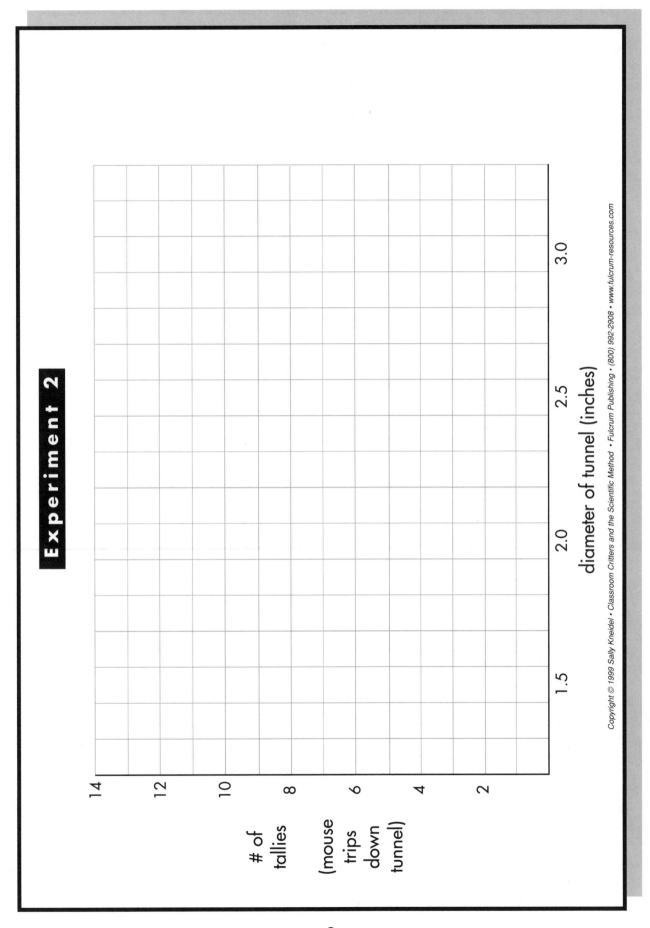

Experiment 2

# of tallies

(mouse trips down tunnel)

14   12   10   8   6   4   2

1.5   2.0   2.5   3.0

diameter of tunnel (inches)

Copyright © 1999 Sally Kneidel • Classroom Critters and the Scientific Method • Fulcrum Publishing • (800) 992-2908 • www.fulcrum-resources.com

Name: _____

Experiment 2

Question: Do mice prefer tunnels of a particular diameter?

Hypothesis: I think the mice will prefer _____

_____

_____

Materials: _____   _____

_____   _____

Procedure: We offered the mouse all four tunnels at once. We tallied how many trips the mouse made down each tunnel.

Results:

tunnel diameter	tallies of trips down tunnel	total	class total

Conclusion: _____

_____

_____

_____

_____

_____

Copyright © 1999 Sally Kneidel • Classroom Critters and the Scientific Method • Fulcrum Publishing • (800) 992-2908 • www.fulcrum-resources.com

Experiment 3

Question

Do Mice Prefer Tunnels (Tubes) Open on One End or Two?

Hypothesis

I think mice will enter the tubes with _____ opening(s) more than the tubes with _____ opening(s).

Materials

- one mouse, hamster, or gerbil per group of children
- one empty terrarium per animal, at least 10 by 15 inches (25 cm x 38 cm), with a lid (unless animals are to be watched constantly)
- two toilet-paper tubes per animal, or a paper towel tube cut in half
- construction paper or cardboard to close off one end of one of the two tubes
- tape for the construction paper or cardboard

Procedure

Each terrarium should have only one test animal and two tubes. One of the tubes will be open on both ends (will have two "doors"). The other tube will have only one door, or one opening. On the second tube, close off one opening by taping a circle of paper or cardboard over it. Don't use foil or shiny tape, which could attract the animal's attention. I usually do this experiment by offering the one-door tube and the two-door tube to the test animal at the same time. If you do it this way, put the tubes side by side in the center of the terrarium so the terrarium walls don't block access to either tube.

Another option is to offer the tubes one at a time. If you do this, alternate which one is offered first in different trials.

With both methods, record how many trips the test animal makes down each tube in a 5-minute period. I tell the children to tally any entry in which at least half the animal's body is in the tube, even if he backs out. However you decide to treat partial entries, be sure the experimenters are consistent.

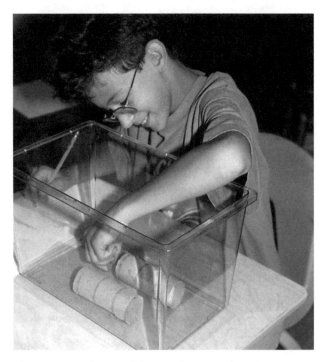

The mouse peeks out of the two-door tunnel as Grant reaches in to adjust the tunnel's position.

Do at least three trials of 5 minutes each, or six trials if you offer the two tubes separately.

If you have several groups of children, each with their own terrarium, tubes, and mouse, then each group can do just one 5-minute trial.

Results

The children record their tallies on the data sheet. They add the number of tallies for their mouse and record the totals in the two "total" blanks. In a class setting, I then go around and call on each group to give me their group totals, which I write on the board. We add them and enter the sums in the two "class total" blanks.

In my experience, the animals enter the two-door tubes about twice as often as the one-door tubes.

Conclusion

You can start a discussion of the results by asking about chipmunk or ground squirrel holes the children may have seen. What do they think happens if a dog or a fox or some other predator digs into the tunnel leading to the rodent's burrow? Is the chipmunk doomed?

Someone may volunteer the information that most or all mammals that live in underground burrows have at least two tunnels to the outside. Can the children say why? How would this help the animal survive? (Every trait in nature has some survival value.)

What about public buildings? I'm sure building codes require at least two exits. Can the children guess why?

So one conclusion here is that the test animals prefer tubes with two doors because of a survival instinct that helps them avoid getting trapped.

Is there another conclusion? See the first Extension.

Identifying the Experimental Concepts

The **experimental variable** in this experiment is the number of openings in the tube. We are interested in the effect of the number of openings on the animal's selection.

The **control** here is having a two-door tube and a one-door tube; there is no difference between the two except for the number of openings. If we had only the two-door tube present, we couldn't say anything about the animal's preference for it in relation to the one-door tube, or vice versa. Having both present allows us to compare, with each as a control for the other.

The **dependent variable** is the number of entries into each tube type. This number varies, depending on the type of tube being considered.

The **controlled variables** are all the other factors that could affect the animal's choice: placement of the tubes, tube size, tube color, tube texture, and so on. All these factors are controlled, or are not allowed to vary.

The need for **multiple trials** here is addressed by offering the choice of tubes in three separate 5-minute trials, for a single animal. If there are several animals, even more multiples are added by compiling the group totals to get class totals.

Extension

Back in the Conclusion section, we said there could be another tentative conclusion, or explanation. What if the test animals are entering the two-door tubes twice as often because they have available to them two ways to enter the two-door tube, but only one way to enter the one-door tube. In other words, in the terrarium they have three doors available to them. One is into a one-door tube, and two of them are into a two-door tube.

Can the children think of any way to address this possible explanation? One option is to offer the test animals two one-door tubes and one two-door tube.

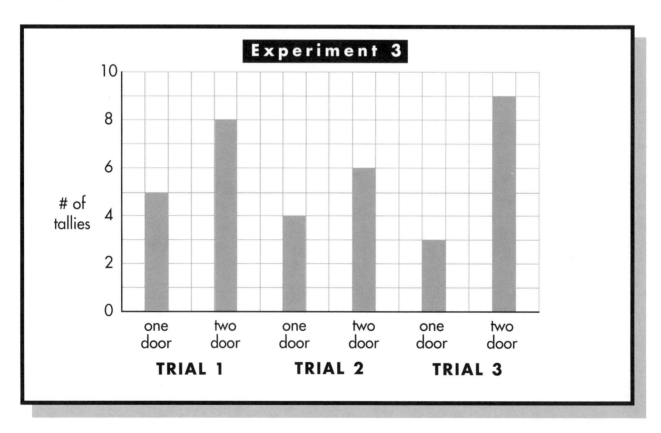

Experiment 3—One possible outcome, using one mouse per trial.

Then they'd have four doors, two of which would be dead ends and two of which would not.

The experimental variable here would still be the number of openings per tube.

Extension

Another offshoot is to make a three-door tube by cutting a circular hole in the side of one tube and inserting the end of another tube. You could offer it with the two-hole tube, or the one-hole tube, or both, or each separately. In this experiment, the experimental variable would again be the number of openings per tube.

Extension

You could vary the experiment by offering any single tube or combination of tubes to more than one animal.

Does having company affect the number of entries made by the original animal? You can mark the fur on the top of his head with a tiny bit of Wite-out or a colored marker. The experimental variable here would be the effect of company on the number of entries.

Extension

Does familiarity with one of the tubes affect the animal's choice? Expose him to one of the tubes before the experiment, only briefly. He will begin to destroy it soon, so keep an eye on him. Ten minutes may be long enough. If you offer only the familiar tube and another identical but unfamiliar tube at the same time, the experimental variable is familiarity with the tube.

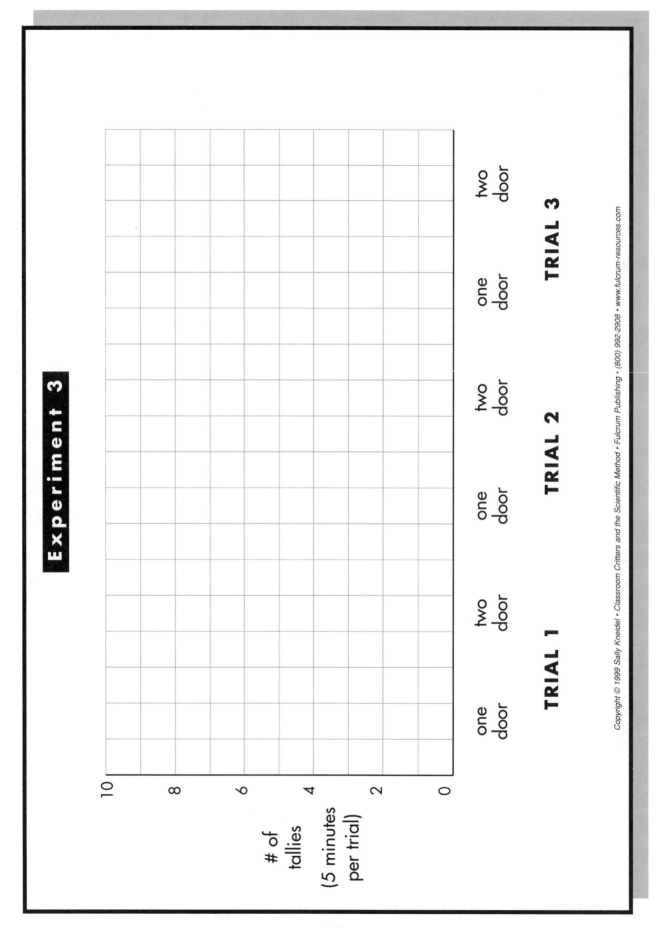

Experiment 3

of
tallies
(5 minutes
per trial)

	one door	two door	one door	two door	one door	two door
	TRIAL 1		TRIAL 2		TRIAL 3	

Copyright © 1999 Sally Kneidel • Classroom Critters and the Scientific Method • Fulcrum Publishing • (800) 992-2908 • www.fulcrum-resources.com

Name: _____

Experiment 3

Question: Do mice prefer tunnels (tubes) open on one end or two?

Hypothesis: I think mice prefer _____

_____

Materials: _____   _____

_____   _____

Procedure: We put the two tubes into the center of the terrarium. Then we introduced the mouse into the terrarium. We tallied how many times the mouse entered each
tunnel over a 5-minute period. We repeated the procedure for two more 5-minute periods,
with rest intervals in between.

Results:

tube type	tallies of mouse entries	total	class total
one door	_____	_____	_____
two door	_____	_____	_____

Conclusion: _____

_____

_____

_____

_____

_____

_____

Copyright © 1999 Sally Kneidel • *Classroom Critters and the Scientific Method* • Fulcrum Publishing • (800) 992-2908 • www.fulcrum-resources.com

Experiment 4

Question

How Fast Can a Rodent Learn to Make the "Correct" Turn Consistently, to Find a Food Treat, in a T-Maze?

Hypothesis

I think mice will learn to go toward a food treat consistently after _____ runs through a T-maze.

Materials

- a sheet of stiff cardboard at least 19 inches by 15 inches (48 cm x 38 cm) (If you plan to use the same maze for Experiment 5 also, start with a piece of cardboard 21 inches by 15 inches instead.)
- more cardboard to make the walls of the maze
- one ruler or meter stick
- one mouse, hamster, or gerbil per maze
- one glue gun
- one pair of scissors
- one data sheet and pencil per child
- healthy snack

Procedure

You'll be making a T-shaped passageway, with cardboard walls glued to the sheet of cardboard. The corridor should be about 3 inches (8 cm) wide. The walls should be about 6 inches (15 cm) tall. The vertical part of the T will be about 12 inches (30 cm) long, and the crosspiece of the T about 12 inches (30 cm) long. So you'll need three pieces of cardboard that are 6 inches (15 cm) by 12 inches (30 cm) for the three uninterrupted walls, and two pieces that are about 4.5 inches (11 cm) by 6 inches (15 cm) for the bottom wall of the crosspiece. Children can do the measuring and possibly the cutting; small errors won't matter.

Draw the T-shaped maze on the flat cardboard before anything is glued. Then use the glue gun to put the walls in place. Don't forget to glue the two seams where the walls meet each other. You may want to reinforce those two corners with a piece of tape on the outside.

Alan and Grant introduce the mouse to the bottom of the cardboard T-maze. The maze is held together with glue from a hot glue gun.

I keep the glue gun plugged in while conducting the experiment, because children bump walls and some walls may get knocked down. With the glue gun already hot, a loose wall can be repaired in seconds.

You'll need to have at least one child per maze who's not afraid to pick up the animal, to restart him. To prevent any escapes, you may want to put each maze inside a short cardboard box. Or you can just have a small box to hold the animal while questions are asked or problems addressed.

This could be a whole group activity with the maze in the center of a circle of children. I have used a small plastic wading pool as an experimental arena. It prevents escape and the sides are low enough to see over. This experiment also works well with one maze and one mouse per group of four. Or a single child at home easily can do the whole thing alone.

You'll need to get some baseline data, for a control, before you offer the reward at one end of the maze. You need to demonstrate that without a reward the test animal chooses both directions equally. It takes ten runs to show this; it may take twenty. Save this data for use as a control in Experiment 5.

Here's how to do the control: Put the animal gently in place at the bottom of the vertical part of the T, with his head and neck inside the corridor, and let him go. If he tries to turn around, the children may turn him back gently. He may be encouraged by gentle prods to go forward, as long as his choice of which way to turn is not influenced. Each time he emerges from the top of the T, the children tally his choice of direction. As long as his head has emerged, that counts. If he tries to go back in, goose him out. Let the children take turns restarting him.

Before starting the next part of the experiment, let the children figure out a healthy snack that your animal really likes. Low-sugar cereals, such as Cheerios or Kix, are favorites. And mice really do like cheese. You may want to call a vet or a pet store for other suggestions. Offer only a small piece after each run of the maze. The animal may fill up fast. If he isn't interested in the treat, remove the food from his cage for two hours before trying the experiment.

The food, or reward, will be offered on one side of the maze consistently. Have the children decide which side, and put the food in place, about 1 inch (2.5 cm) beyond the last edge of the crosspiece wall.

Then repeat the procedure described above for the control. Plan on doing twenty runs through the maze with each animal, or set a time limit instead, of perhaps 10 minutes. It'll be easier to compare the control trials (no reward) to the trials with a reward if you use the same number of runs or the same amount of time for each. If you didn't, you can compare proportions or percents. (For example, "In the control, he turned right 52 percent of the time, but with the reward, he turned right 90 percent of the time.)

Results

In my experience, rodents in a T-maze with no reward have no directional preference. They turn both ways equally. But they learn very quickly in a maze with a reward to turn toward the food every time. After discovering the food, some animals will make no errors or "wrong" turns at all.

In writing about this experiment, a "Results" section will include the number of tallies for each directional choice for the control (no reward) and for the trials with a reward. This will be four numbers: right and left turns for the control, and right and left turns for the reward trials. If the children worked in groups, these will be the group totals. If the experiment is conducted in groups within a class, you may want to add the group totals for each of the four categories to arrive at class totals.

The results section also includes any relevant observations, such as, "At first the mouse kept standing on his hind legs and sniffing the wall."

Conclusion

The children accept or reject their own hypotheses here. They also try to explain their result in terms of how it affects the animal's survival. Food has obvious survival value. The ability to learn quickly is characteristic of most mammals. Rodents, in particular, often store food and must have the ability to remember where it is.

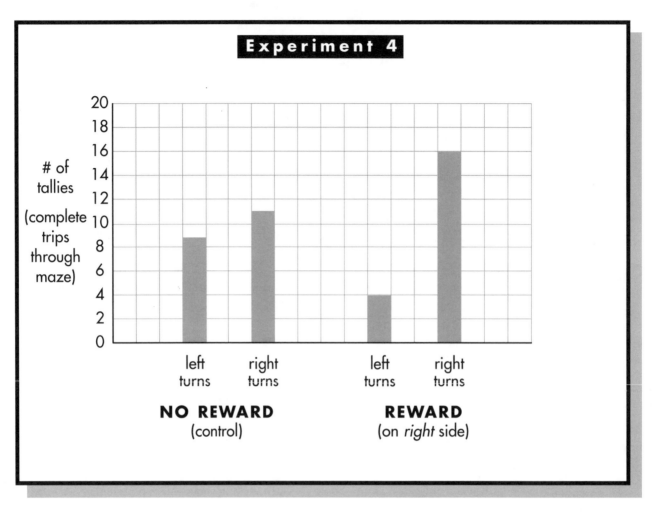

Experiment 4—One possible outcome, for twenty runs with no reward (the control) and twenty runs with a reward on the right side of the maze.

Identifying the Experimental Concepts

The **experimental variable** in this experiment is the presence and location of the food reward. We're asking about the effect of the reward on the animal's choice of directions.

The trials done with no reward serve as the **control** here. If we didn't do those trials, we wouldn't know for sure that the animal didn't have an innate tendency to turn in one direction, or that he wasn't turning toward sunlight or something else.

The **dependent variable** in this experiment is the number of turns in each direction when a reward is offered. Those numbers depend upon which side has the reward.

The **controlled variables** are the other factors, besides a food reward, that could affect the mouse's choice. The same maze must be used for control and reward trials. Experimenter behavior (noise, bumping, gesturing, etc.) should be consistent throughout. The two ends of the T crosspiece should open into comparable areas so that the rodent gets roughly similar views when standing at the top of the T, deciding which way to go. If he sees children's faces at the end of one corridor, he should see children's faces the other way as well.

The need for **multiple repetitions** is addressed in this experiment by having the animal make ten or twenty runs for the control, and ten or twenty runs for a reward.

Extension

Now that you know how one particular food treat affects the animal's choice in the maze, you can investigate the reward value of other things. What other foods motivate the animal to turn one way consistently? Can anything besides food have that effect? Play objects? Another animal of the same species? Another animal of a different species? (Be wary of fights.)

Extension

Is there anything not dangerous to your test animal that could repel him, or cause him to turn the *opposite* direction consistently? What if you put a cotton ball with a tiny bit of dilute ammonia on it at one end of the maze? (Ammonia can damage eyes; don't let children handle it or breathe it deeply.) What if you blow a shrill whistle every time he comes out the left side of the maze? Or clap your hands in the air right over his head?

Extension

How long does the test animal retain what he learned? If you run him through the maze the next day without a reward, will he turn toward where the food was before? What if you wait three days? A week? Three weeks?

The mouse emerges from the right side of the T-maze.

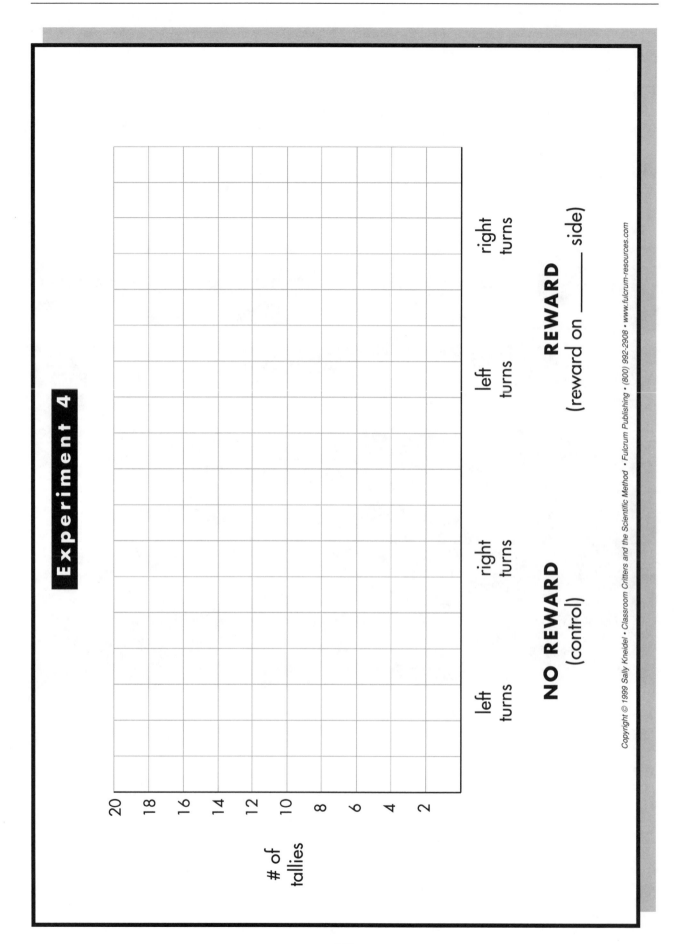

Copyright © 1999 Sally Kneidel • *Classroom Critters and the Scientific Method* • Fulcrum Publishing • (800) 992-2908 • www.fulcrum-resources.com

Name: _____

Experiment 4

Question: How fast can a rodent learn to make the "correct" turn consistently, to find a food treat, in a T-maze?

Hypothesis: I think mice will learn to go toward the treat consistently after _____ runs through a T-maze.

Materials: _____   _____

_____   _____

Procedure: A T-shaped maze was constructed with cardboard and a glue gun. The animal was placed at the bottom of the T and allowed to run through the maze _____ times. Each time we tallied which way the animal turned at the top of the maze. Then we allowed the animal to run through the maze _____ more times, this time with a reward (_____) at the opening on the left side at the top of the T. We replaced the reward each time it was eaten. Again, we tallied which way the animal turned each time.

Results:	tallies of left turns	total	tallies of right turns	total
no reward on either side	_____	_____	_____	_____
reward at opening on left	_____	_____	_____	_____

Conclusion: _____

_____

_____

_____

_____

Copyright © 1999 Sally Kneidel • Classroom Critters and the Scientific Method • Fulcrum Publishing • (800) 992-2908 • www.fulcrum-resources.com

Experiment 5

Question

Will a Mouse Consistently Alternate Directions in a Forced-Turn Maze?

Hypothesis

I think a mouse that is forced to turn left in a maze will, at the second turn, (a) usually turn right, (b) usually turn left, or (c) turn left and right equally.

Materials

- a sheet of stiff cardboard at least 18 inches by 15 inches (45 cm x 38 cm) or the T-maze from Experiment 4
- more cardboard to make the walls of the maze, or to add more walls to the T-maze
- one ruler or meter stick
- one mouse, hamster, or gerbil per maze
- one glue gun
- one pair of scissors
- one data sheet and pencil per child

Procedure

The data you collected for the control in Experiment 4 can serve as a control here too. If you didn't do Experiment 4, follow the instructions there on how to make a plain T-maze. As a control for both Experiments 4 and 5, the children need to establish that the test animals have no innate preference for right or left at a T intersection. If a mouse runs through a T-maze twenty times with no reward or other influence, he'll turn left approximately ten times and right ten times.

This experiment easily can be done by one child with one animal. If you have a class of children and several animals and mazes, groups of four work well. To prevent animal escapes, either put each maze in a cardboard box, or have a smaller box or old margarine tub to hold each animal while instructions are given.

If you have only one animal but a lot of children, you can put the maze in a low plastic wading pool. The children can form two concentric circles around the pool, first row seated, second row

Chekeya and Joanne look on as Jessica introduces the mouse to the entry of a forced-right-turn maze.

standing, so that everyone can see. But small groups are better. Another option if you have only one animal but a class of children is to have groups work consecutively, with each group doing a few runs through the maze.

For the control, do at least ten to twenty total runs through the maze, depending on time available. It may take twenty to show that there is no directional preference. Have the children enter the number of right turns and the number of left turns on the data sheet.

Once you've finished collecting the data for the control, you can alter the maze to do the "forced-turn" trials. You'll need to add another short sideways passage to the bottom of the T so that the maze now looks like a T with an L superimposed on it. The sideways passage can project to the right, as in the letter L, or to the left as in a backwards L. To add this leg of the maze, cut away about 3 inches (8 cm) of wall length at the base of the T, on one side only. This new space is the door into the new addition. You'll need two new pieces of cardboard for the new walls, one about 4.5 iches (11cm) long and one about 7.5 inches (19 cm) long, each about 6 inches (15 cm) tall to match the other walls. Glue the new walls in position with a glue gun.

To begin, put the animal in place at the bottom of the maze, with his head and neck inside the corridor, and let him go. He may be gently encouraged if he stalls, but no prodding is allowed to influence his choice of direction at the top of the T. Repeat this procedure about twenty times. If you have five groups, then each group need do it only four times. But the children will want to do it more than that. The more data they have, the more convincing their results.

Results

In this section, the children record the number of left and right turns in the control (T-maze, no reward), and the number of left and right turns in the forced-turn maze. If they've worked in groups, have them record group totals. Then let representatives of each group announce each group's totals. Have the children add the group totals to arrive at class totals. Also record in this section any relevant observations of the animals' behavior, or external events that could have affected their behavior, such as, "Robert kept whispering into the left side of the T and scaring the mouse."

Conclusion

Here the children attempt to explain and make sense of their results. An animal that alternates directions in any two turns is going to follow more or less a straight line, albeit a zigzag straight line. A straight or zigzag line will enable him to cover some ground if he's seeking food or protection. An animal that chooses the same direction in any two turns is going to go around in circles. So there is some advantage to alternating directions. Mealworms apparently have a genetic tendency to alternate directions. Mammals have fewer programmed behaviors than insects, and more choices based on judgment or prior experience or momentary whim. A number of factors could affect a rodent's decision.

Identifying the Experimental Concepts

The **experimental variable** here is the presence or absence of the forced turn upon entering the T-maze. We're looking at the effect of the forced turn on the animal's choice at the T intersection.

The **control** in this experiment is the first series of trials using the T-maze before the L is added.

The **dependent variable** is the number of left and right turns at the T after passing the L or forced turn. These counts depend upon the presence or absence of the forced turn.

The **controlled variables** are all the things that could affect the animal's choice of direction, but that are held steady to avoid influencing the choice. The two mazes must be identical other than the presence or absence of the additional turn. All trials must be conducted in the same place, at the same time of day, with the same amount of disturbance, and so on.

The need for **multiple trials** is met by allowing the animal to run down the maze several times without the extra turn and with the extra turn.

Extension

One extension is to alter the direction of the added passageway onto the maze, so that in some trials the animal must turn left to enter the long run of the T and in some trials he must turn right to enter it. Do mirror-image mazes produce mirror-image behavior? The experimental variable would be the direction of the first turn, the forced turn.

Extension

Does varying the distance between turns alter the influence that the first turn has on the second turn? Using mealworms, this distance does make a difference. The shorter the distance, the stronger the influence the first turn has on the direction taken at the second turn. Here the experimental variable would be the distance.

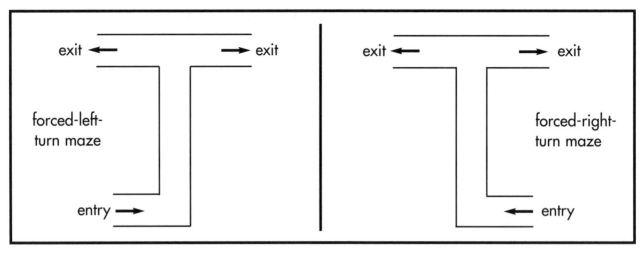

Examples of a forced-left- and forced-right-turn maze.

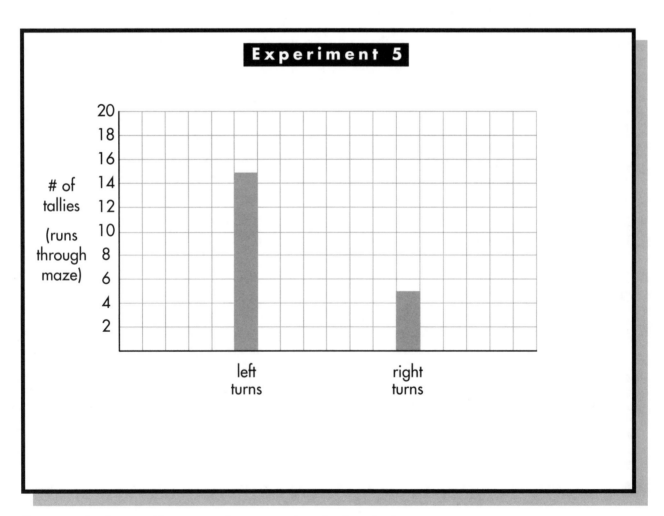

Experiment 5—One possible outcome of twenty runs through a forced-right-turn maze.

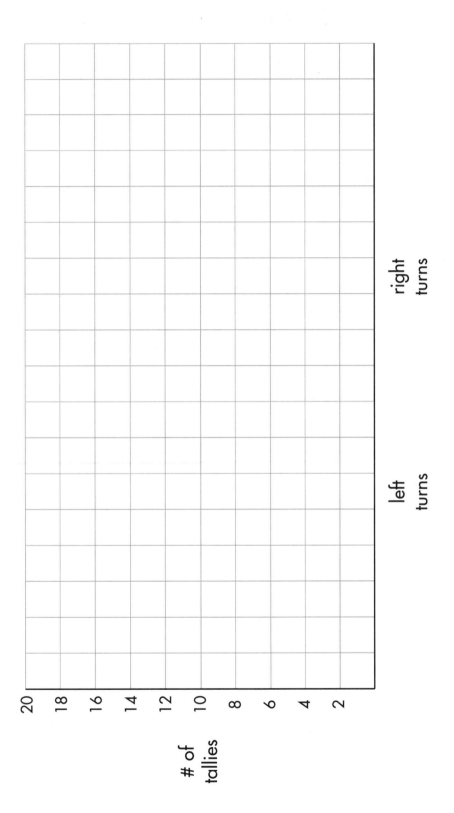

Experiment 5

# of tallies

20 18 16 14 12 10 8 6 4 2

left turns

right turns

Copyright © 1999 Sally Kneidel • Classroom Critters and the Scientific Method • Fulcrum Publishing • (800) 992-2908 • www.fulcrum-resources.com

Name: _____

Experiment 5

Question: Will a mouse consistently alternate directions in a forced-turn maze?

Hypothesis: I think _____

_____

Materials:_____ _____

_____ _____

Procedure: A T-shaped maze was constructed with cardboard and a glue gun. The animal was placed at the bottom of the T and allowed to run through the maze _____ times. Each time we tallied which way the mouse turned at the top of the maze. Then we added an additional corridor at the bottom of the T so that the animal was forced to turn right to enter the T. Again, starting the animal at the bottom each time, we allowed it to run through the forced-turn maze _____ times. Each time we tallied which way it turned at the top.

Results:

tallies of left turns in T-maze	total	class total		tallies of right turns in T-maze	total	class total

tallies of left turns in forced-turn maze	total	class total		tallies of right turns in forced-turn maze	total	class total

Conclusion: _____

_____

_____

Copyright © 1999 Sally Kneidel • *Classroom Critters and the Scientific Method* • Fulcrum Publishing • (800) 992-2908 • www.fulcrum-resources.com

Experiment 6

Question

How Does a Food Reward Affect a Mouse's Performance in a Complex Maze?

Hypothesis

I think rewarding the mouse at the end of the maze will / will not affect the number of errors the mouse makes.

I think the mouse will make _____ errors in a maze with four choices, before reaching the

_____.

Materials

- one mouse (in my experience, gerbils do not perform as well as mice do in mazes)
- a flat board or piece of thick cardboard, about 18 inches by 18 inches
- several strips of thick cardboard, 12 to 18 inches (30 to 45 cm) long and 6 or 7 inches (15 to 18 cm) wide
- a hot glue gun
- scissors for shortening the cardboard strips as needed

Procedure

Draw a maze on the cardboard sheet or board. Use the design provided or make up your own. The corridors should be at least 2.5 inches (6.4 cm) wide, or a little wider if you like. Consider the size of the animal you'll be working with. The walls should be about 6 inches (15 cm) tall, or taller if you know your animal can jump higher. Cut the strips of cardboard to match the lengths of the walls you've drawn. Then use the glue gun to put the walls in place. Don't forget to glue the seams where the walls meet each other. You may want to reinforce those corners with a piece of tape.

Note: I keep the glue gun plugged in while conducting the experiment, because children bump walls and some may get knocked down. But with the glue gun already hot, a loose wall can be repaired in seconds.

If you have only one mouse, you'll need to do the control first. Introduce a mouse to the beginning of

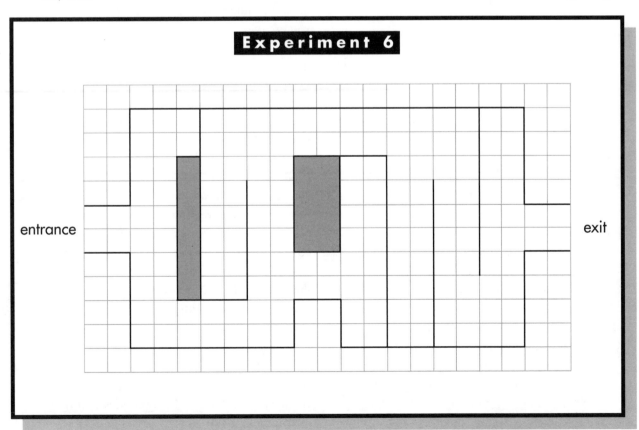

Experiment 6—One possible maze design.

the maze. Make a tally mark every time the mouse chooses any direction other than the one leading most directly to the maze exit. When he gets to the end, wait a couple of minutes then start him over at the beginning. Repeat this procedure five more times, recording the number of errors made in each run.

For the experimental trials, put a small mouse treat at the end of the maze. Introduce a mouse to the beginning of the maze. Make a tally mark every time the mouse chooses any direction other than the one leading most directly to the treat. If the mouse used in the control trials improved his performance (reduced the number of mistakes) with practice, even though he wasn't rewarded, then you probably need to get another mouse for the experimental runs. You'll want your mouse to make a lot of mistakes in the beginning of the experimental trials so he'll have a lot of room for improvement.

After the mouse has successfully gotten to the treat, let him eat it. Then start the mouse over at the beginning of the maze, and place another treat at the end. Repeat this procedure until the mouse has run the maze six times.

Results

Your results will be the number of errors made in each run or trial, for both the control and the experimental trials (with treats). Most mice make ten to sixteen errors on every run with no reward. With a reward, they'll make a lot of errors on the first run, and fewer errors on each successive run. By the sixth run with a reward, some mice are down to only one or two errors.

Conclusion

In this section, you either accept or reject your hypothesis, thereby answering the original question. You also attempt to explain the results. In this case, we've shown that mice can learn if they are motivated to learn, if they have something to gain by learning. Many or most vertebrates can learn, and a lot of invertebrates can too. For humans, learning is often its own reward. We often enjoy knowledge for its own sake. Animals are more likely to require a food reward, or some other positive or negative stimulus. In humans,

rewarding students with candy actually tends to interfere with learning, diverting attention from the lesson to the candy.

Identifying the Experimental Concepts

The **experimental variable** here is the presence or absence of a reward at the end of the maze. We're examining the effect of a reward on the number of mistakes made.

The **control** in this experiment is having the mouse go through the maze both with and without treats. We couldn't say anything about the effect of a reward on learning unless we also tried it without a reward. If you're really just curious about how many mistakes the mouse will make at first, or how many runs he'll do before he improves, then you can skip the control runs and use a reward every time.

The **dependent variable** here is the number of mistakes the mouse makes. We're guessing, or hypothesizing, that the mouse will eventually learn to make fewer mistakes in order to get to the reward faster.

The **controlled variables** are all the factors that could have affected the mouse's progress through the maze but didn't because we kept them the same. If you use two or more mice for the experiment, try to be consistent with age and gender if you can. Keep distractions consistent, use the same treat for all trials, keep the maze the same, and so on.

To have **multiple trials** in this experiment, you'll need to repeat the entire procedure at least twice more. You'll need at least two additional mice for the control, and two additional mice for the experimental runs with a reward. I don't know that you really need multiple trials here for an informal experiment. You're already doing six runs for a single experimental trial and six runs for the control. If your mouse steadily improves in the experimental trial with a reward, and doesn't in the control, then the results are pretty convincing already. But if his behavior is hard to interpret, additional trials will help clarify your results.

Extension

After watching the mouse go through the maze, do you have a feel for how many choices or turns the mouse could handle before he would fail to ever reach the exit? Does doubling the number of choices double

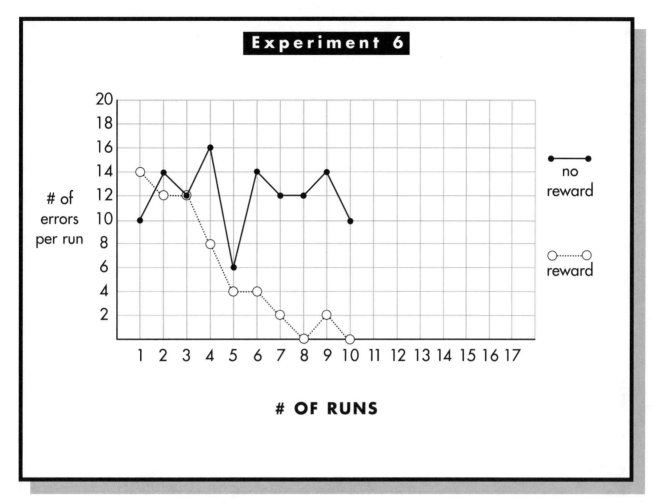

Experiment 6

of errors per run

OF RUNS

no reward

reward

Experiment 6—One possible outcome of ten runs with a reward and ten runs without a reward.

the number of minutes it takes him to reach the exit? Or does he give up?

Extension

Is there anything other than food that will reward him, that will cause him to move through the maze more quickly? Will a mother mouse learn to move through more quickly if her baby is at the other end? Will a male mouse move through more quickly if a female mouse is at the other end? What kinds of foods are rewarding for mice? Broccoli? Chicken? Potato chips?

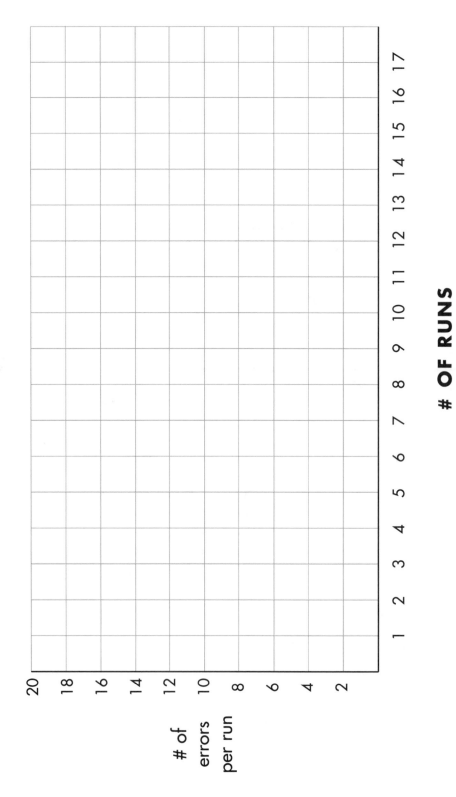

Experiment 6

# of errors per run

20 18 16 14 12 10 8 6 4 2

1 2 3 4 5 6 7 8 9 10 11 12 13 14 15 16 17

OF RUNS

Copyright © 1999 Sally Kneidel • Classroom Critters and the Scientific Method • Fulcrum Publishing • (800) 992-2908 • www.fulcrum-resources.com

Name: _____

Experiment 6

Question: How does a food reward affect a mouse's performance in a complex maze?

Hypothesis: I think _____

_____

Materials: _____   _____

_____   _____

Procedure: We constructed a maze of cardboard. We allowed a mouse to run through the maze _____ times. Each time it ran through we counted the number of errors it made before exiting the maze. Then we repeated the above procedure, this time placing a food reward at the "out" door for each run.

Results:

Number of errors per trial with no reward (Control trials)

Number of errors per trial with reward (Experimental trials)

Trial #	# errors		Trial #	# errors
1	_____		1	_____
2	_____		2	_____
3	_____		3	_____
4	_____		4	_____
5	_____		5	_____
6	_____		6	_____

Conclusion: _____

_____

_____

Copyright © 1999 Sally Kneidel • Classroom Critters and the Scientific Method • Fulcrum Publishing • (800) 992-2908 • www.fulcrum-resources.com

Experiment 7

Question

Which Is Faster—Hamster, Gerbil, or Mouse?

Hypothesis

I think the hamster / gerbil / mouse will be fastest.

Materials

- one hamster
- one gerbil
- one mouse
- one sheet of poster paper
- one dark marker
- one large trash can lid to trace around (optional)
- one coffee can or clear jar to trace around (optional)
- one clock with a second hand

Procedure

This is a particularly easy experiment to set up for several groups. All you need for each group is an animal and a racetrack. The children can make their own racetracks. Using the dark marker, the children will trace around the trash can lid to make a large circle on a piece of poster paper. The circle should be almost as wide as the poster paper. Using a meter stick, they can locate the center of the circle and mark it with a pencil. In the center of the large circle, have them draw a smaller circle by tracing around the coffee can. Now their racetracks are ready.

If each group of children has one animal, then each group can race its animal singly against the clock. If you have more animals, then racing them in pairs is an option, but only if the animals are familiar with each other. Unacquainted animals may fight. To answer the question posed by the experiment title, you could let two groups use hamsters, two groups use gerbils, and two groups use mice.

For each trial in a group of four, two students per group can be clock-watchers while the other two watch the animal. The poster paper with the racetrack can rest on top of the juncture of the four desks. To begin a trial, an appointed child in each group will place a single animal in the center of the small circle. When everyone is ready and focused, the animal handler says "Go" and releases the animal. When the animal crosses the line of the inner circle, the two animal watchers say "Start counting." The clock-watchers then note the position of the second hand on the clock, and one keeps watching the clock while the other writes the time down. When the animal crosses the line of the outer circle, the animal watchers say "Stop." The clock-watchers note the position of the second hand, and both write down the time. The animal handler returns the animal to its cage or holds it temporarily. The group members figure out the number of seconds that

The gerbil bolts from the starting circle as soon as the enclosure that held it in the center is lifted. Nate starts the timer, and Katie gets ready to record the finishing time.

The hamster looks around cautiously, in hamster fashion, before setting off. Nate clutches the enclosure that kept the hamster in the center, Jonathan starts the timer, and Katie looks on.

elapsed and record it. If someone has a stopwatch on his or her wristwatch, you'll have fewer errors in measuring the time.

You may want to let each group do four trials so that each child has the opportunity to release the animal inside the small circle. They can use the same animal four times. Most of the time the animal will not go in a straight line, but that doesn't matter. After all four trials have been run, the children can identify which trial was fastest, which was slowest, calculate the total of the four, and/or calculate the average of the four. I usually make an overhead of the data sheet and call on each group to tell me their fastest time, which I record in the group data blocks. If we're studying means and medians, I may ask for one of those instead. Or I may ask for all four of each group's measurements.

If you want to do this as a whole group activity, you can put the racetrack on the floor, perhaps in a child's wading pool. Half the children can kneel in a circle around the pool while the other half stands behind them.

Results

Gerbils and mice are often faster than hamsters. Gerbils, in particular, sometimes bolt from the starting circle. Hamsters may spend more time sitting before starting out. The children should record their time measurements in the "Results" section, as well as any relevant observations.

Conclusion

The students should try to make sense of their results, to explain the results if they can. Are mice and gerbils really faster than hamsters, or simply more active? Were some of the animals bigger than others? Older than others? Sleepier than others? These factors should be evened out, or controlled for, in the beginning if possible, but it isn't always possible.

Identifying the Experimental Concepts

The **experimental variable** here is the species of animal. We're looking at the effect of species identity on speed.

The plastic pool is useful for playing with the animals as well as for experiments.

The identity of the **control** in this experiment depends upon your perspective. If you're looking at the speed of mice in relation to the speed of hamsters, then the speed of hamsters is your control; but if you're looking at the speed of hamsters in relation to the speed of gerbils, then the speed of gerbils is your control.

The **dependent variable** is the speed of the test animal. We're supposing, or hypothesizing, that the speed of the animal depends upon which species it is—hamster, gerbil, or mouse. It may turn out, however, that the variation within each species is greater than the variation between species.

The **controlled variables** are all the factors that could affect the animal's speed but which we tried to keep steady, such as animal age, size, hunger, and restedness. If all the gerbils are babies, and all the mice are old and obese, the results could be due to age and obesity rather than species.

The need for **multiple trials** is met by having each group do at least one trial. If your're doing this experiment as an individual or a whole group activity, you would need to do at least three trials.

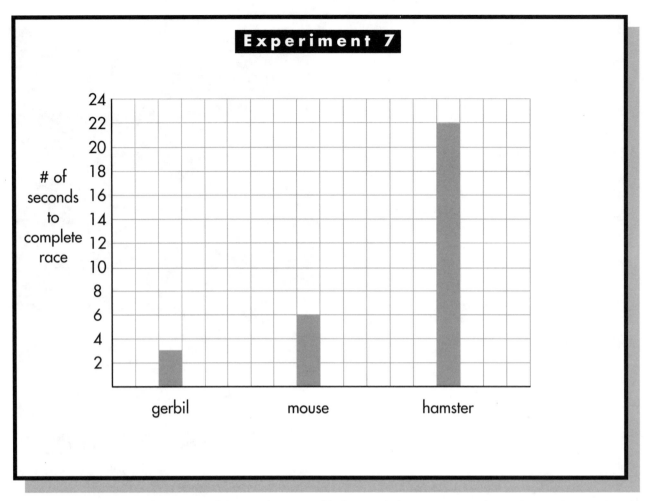

Experiment 7

Experiment 7—One possible outcome of three trials. You could also graph the average time for each animal, over several trials.

Extension

The children can test for consistent individual differences within one species. If you have a pair of hamsters, is one usually faster than the other?

Extension

Are there factors other than species that are good predictors of speed? Are animals consistently faster in getting across the finish line in the early morning than in the afternoon? Is animal size a good predictor? Does having the racetrack contained within a wading pool affect the animals' speed? (A wide open horizon may spur them to wander faster than the sight of nearby walls.)

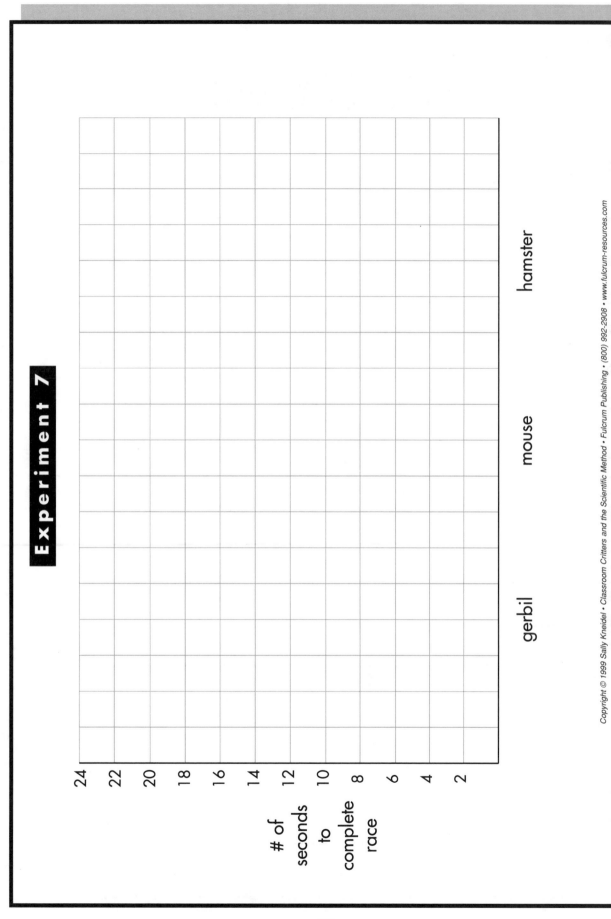

Experiment 7

of
seconds
to
complete
race

24 22 20 18 16 14 12 10 8 6 4 2

gerbil   mouse   hamster

Copyright © 1999 Sally Kneidel • Classroom Critters and the Scientific Method • Fulcrum Publishing • (800) 992-2908 • www.fulcrum-resources.com

Name: _____

Experiment 7

Question: Which is faster—hamster, gerbil, or mouse?

Hypothesis: I think _____

_____

Materials:_____ _____

_____ _____

Procedure: We drew a racetrack on poster paper. We placed each animal, singly, into the center of the racetrack. We tested each animal alone, timing how long it took the animal to cross the outer circle. Then we compared times.

Results:

	Hamster # of seconds to complete race	Gerbil # of seconds to complete race	Mouse # of seconds to complete race
trial 1			
trial 2			
trial 3			
trial 4			
fastest time, mean time, or total time			
class mean or total			

Conclusion: _____

_____

_____

Copyright © 1999 Sally Kneidel • Classroom Critters and the Scientific Method • Fulcrum Publishing • (800) 992-2908 • www.fulcrum-resources.com

Sara offers friendly words to the gerbil, which has just been awakened for experimental duties.

Experiment 8

Question
Do Gerbils Seek the Company of Other Gerbils?

Hypothesis
(a) I think Gerbil A will choose the company of Gerbil B rather than solitude.
(b) I think Gerbil A will avoid Gerbil B.
(c) I think Gerbil A will be indifferent to Gerbil B.

Materials
- at least one terrarium with a lid or at least one cardboard box (14 inches by 20 inches or larger, and 15 inches deep to keep the animal from jumping out; that's 35 cm by 50 cm or larger and 38 cm deep)
- a mesh lid if using a shallow box—some sort of sheer cloth or window screening or hardware cloth, to allow visibility but prevent escape
- two gerbils
- one grease pencil or an 18-inch (45 cm) piece of string for marking the midline of the terrarium

Procedure
The above materials are for a single experimenter or a single group. To conduct the experiment with several groups of four, you'll need one terrarium or box per group and two animals per group. A terrarium might work best in this experiment, allowing quick visibility of the animals' positions without disturbing their behavior. Doing the experiment as a whole group activity will require a central location for the terrarium, with the children forming two concentric circles around it. The inner circle may sit while the outer circle kneels or stands.

The terrarium or box that will be the site of the experiment should not be the home of either the test animal or the second animal. All areas of the box should be equally attractive, so the floor must be uniformly bare or uniformly

Joanne, William, and Jessica tally the gerbils' relative positions as Chekeya keeps track of the time. In this photo, the students were tallying the gerbils' positions every 30 seconds instead of every 10 minutes.

covered with pine shavings. There should be no toys, no nest or bed area, and no food or water present during the experiment, unless you place a water container at each end or in the center.

The children will be tallying at regular intervals which half of the terrarium each gerbil is in. So they need to be able to tell unambiguously which half is which. You'll need to make a line on the inside of the terrarium to distinguish one half from the other. On a terrarium with glass walls, you can make two vertical lines, one in the center of each long wall, with a grease pencil. Or you can put masking tape on the glass to mark the midline of each long wall. Another option is to tape a piece of string across the center of the terrarium, like a bridge, so that students looking down will see the string as a dividing line between the two halves. If using a cardboard box, just mark the midline with a crayon or marker. The children can do the measuring required and perhaps the marking too, depending on their ages.

The frequency of tallies depends upon the activity level of Gerbil A. You may want to observe both animals in the test container for a

few minutes before the experiment starts, perhaps on an earlier day, to see how often they cross the midline. Animals introduced to a new container often wander around quite a bit, while rodents in a familiar container may stay in the same spot for hours. What we're really wondering here is whether Gerbil A will choose to settle next to Gerbil B after he's had enough wandering around. Or whether Gerbil A will choose to avoid Gerbil B, or will just ignore Gerbil B.

Start by putting both gerbils into the terrarium. Let them wander around for 10 minutes or so to get familiar with their new surroundings. The experiment begins when you decide to start tallying the gerbil's location. Record Gerbil A's position relative to Gerbil B every 10 minutes for an hour. You can reduce the time between tallies if your gerbils are very active. If the animals look identical, you can put a dab of Wite-Out on the back of Gerbil A's head, where he can't reach it to chew it off. Label the two halves of the terrarium as Side 1 and Side 2. When the students tally, they should indicate which animal was in which half of the terrarium. Even though you're only asking about their location relative to each other, not

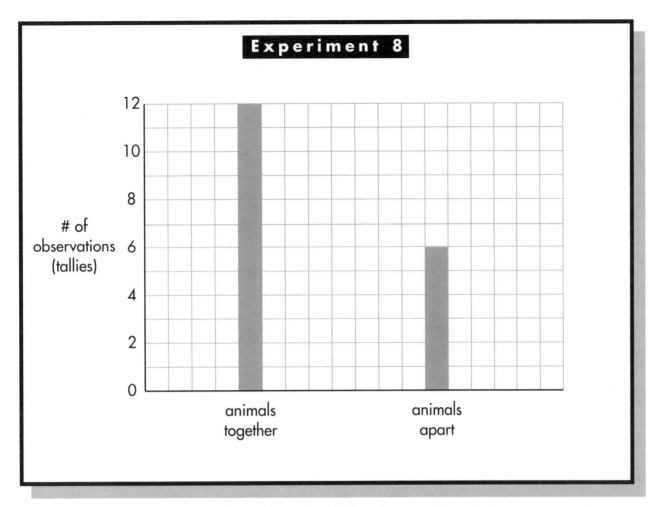

Experiment 8

Experiment 8—One possible outcome, showing the number of tallies of mice together and of mice apart, in eighteen observations.

their frequency of movement; that information may be of interest later if other questions arise.

Unless your examples are very clear-cut, you should probably do at least three trials (three hour-long observation periods).

Example A			Example B			Example C		
	Side 1	Side 2		Side 1	Side 2		Side 1	Side 2
10 min	B	A	10 min	A	B	10 min		AB
20 min	BA		20 min	B	A	20 min	A	B
30 min	BA		30 min	AB		30 min	A	B
40 min	BA		40 min	B	A	40 min	B	A
50 min	B	A	50 min	B	A	50 min		AB
60 min	BA		60 min	B	A	60 min		AB

If one animal is attracted to the other, they will probably be on the same side of the terrarium most of the time (Example A). If either animal is avoiding the other, they will probably be on opposite sides (opposide ends) of the terrarium for most of the tallies (Example B). If they're indifferent to one another, then they should be in opposite sides

or ends of the terrarium about half the time (Example C).

Results

The completed tallies are the results. The children should add up the number of tallies in each category: animals in same half, animals in opposite halves. Similar numbers in the two categories means the animals are probably indifferent to each other. A significantly higher number in the "opposite halves" category means at least one animal is avoiding the other. But if most observations found the animals in the same half, then at least one must be seeking the other's company. Maybe only one of them is doing the seeking, and the other is indifferent. What if one is avoiding company, whereas the other is seeking company? This could make for some interesting results.

Conclusion

In this section, the children attempt to explain the results. Were the animals fighting? Was one rebuffing the other? Was one attempting to mate with the other? Were they going after the two water bottles at opposite ends of the terrarium? Children can usually offer reasons after close observation; they may not be realistic reasons.

Identifying the Experimental Concepts

The **experimental variable** in this experiment is the presence of Gerbil B. We're asking how the presence of a potential companion affects the location of Animal A.

The **control** here is contained within the experimental set up. We're asking whether Animal A chooses the company of Animal B (or tolerates it if B is the seeker of company). Giving Animal A the option of solitude, in the opposite half of the terrarium, is the control.

The **dependent variable** is the location of Gerbil A relative to Gerbil B. That location depends upon the presence of Gerbil B.

The **controlled variables** are all the factors that could influence Gerbil A's choice of location but which are being kept equal between the two halves of the terrarium. Those factors are presence of food, a bed or nest, water, toys, or any other object or animal.

The need for **multiple trials** is met by doing three trials.

Extension

One possible variation of this experiment is to vary the gender of the two animals. Here the experimental variable would be gender.

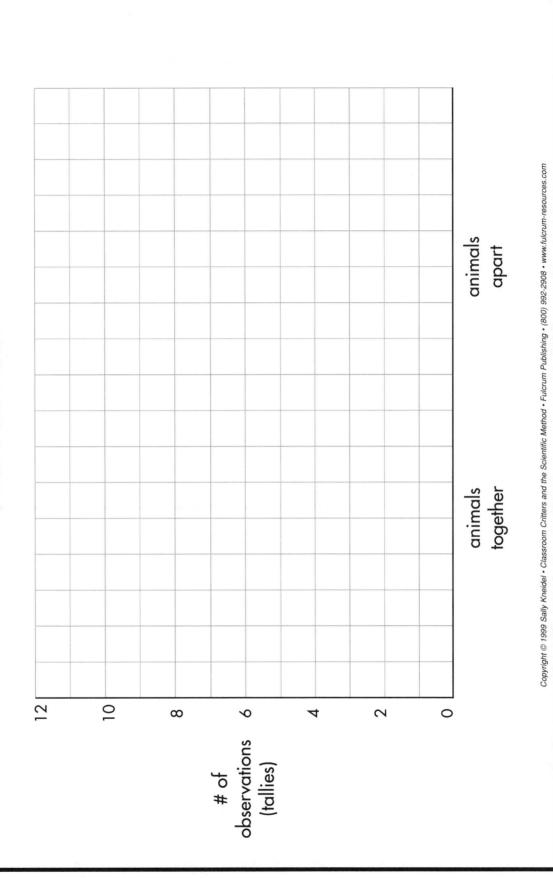

Experiment 8

# of observations (tallies)

animals together

animals apart

12 10 8 6 4 2 0

Copyright © 1999 Sally Kneidel • Classroom Critters and the Scientific Method • Fulcrum Publishing • (800) 992-2908 • www.fulcrum-resources.com

Name: _____

Experiment 8

Question: Do gerbils seek the company of other gerbils?

Hypothesis: I think _____

_____

Materials:_____   _____

_____   _____

Procedure: We divided a terrarium in half by drawing a line across the middle. We labeled the two halves or sides "1" and "2." We put in two gerbils that we could tell apart. In each trial, we checked the positions of the gerbils every 10 minutes for an hour. Each time we checked, we wrote down which half each gerbil was in. We did three trials in all. Then we figured out the number of observations, of eighteen total, where (1) the gerbils were in the same half together and (2) the gerbils were in opposite halves.

Results:

	Trial 1		Trial 2		Trial 3	
	Side 1	Side 2	Side 1	Side 2	Side 1	Side 2
10 minutes	_____	_____	_____	_____	_____	_____
20 minutes	_____	_____	_____	_____	_____	_____
30 minutes	_____	_____	_____	_____	_____	_____
40 minutes	_____	_____	_____	_____	_____	_____
50 minutes	_____	_____	_____	_____	_____	_____
60 minutes	_____	_____	_____	_____	_____	_____

Number of observations when the two gerbils were in the same half:_____ of 18

Number of observations when the two gerbils were in opposite halves:_____ of 18

Which is more? _____ Or are they about the same? _____

Conclusion: _____

_____

Copyright © 1999 Sally Kneidel • Classroom Critters and the Scientific Method • Fulcrum Publishing • (800) 992-2908 • www.fulcrum-resources.com

Experiment 9

Question

Are Male Mice and Female Mice Equally Aggressive Toward Male "Intruders"?

Hypothesis

I think male mice will be more aggressive than / less aggressive than / equally as aggressive as female mice.

Materials

- at least one terrarium with a lid
- two adult male mice
- one adult female mouse
- one piece of stiff cardboard at least 18 inches long and the same width as the terrarium
- food and a food container for mice
- water and a water container for mice
- litter or newspaper for the floor of the terrarium

Procedure

To begin the experiment, put one male mouse in the terrarium. If you plan to have him in there for more than an hour, set up the terrarium as you would if it were his home, with food, water, and shavings or newspaper on the floor of the terrarium. Or you can use his regular cage as the setting of the experiment. Give your mouse at least 10 minutes or so to get used to his new surroundings. Then, lower another male into the cage, holding him by the tail. Quickly remove your hand. Observe what happens. If the mice fight, separate them right away by pressing the lower edge of the cardboard (see "Materials") between them all the way to the floor of the terrarium. Keep it in place as a barrier between the two until they calm down—5 minutes or more. At that time, pick up the intruder by the tail and place him in his original carrier. If he still seems upset after the 5-minute wait, put on a heavy glove before picking him up.

Repeat this two more times, on different days if possible, so that you'll be starting with calm mice each time. Or, ideally, repeat it with different mice.

After you've tested the males together, clean out the test terrarium, set it up as you did before, and put a female in alone. Then repeat the above procedure, introducing a male intruder. Does the female react the same way the male did? Repeat two more times, with different mice or on different days, to be sure your results are reliable.

Results

In my experience, two male mice will fight, whether they are strangers or littermates. The female and an intruding male will not fight. Neither will two females. The children can jot notes on the worksheet about observed behaviors, and perhaps write out a more readable description when the action is over. They can also write on the worksheet the total number of male mice who fought the intruder (probably three) versus the number of female mice fighting the intruder (probably zero). In this experiment, the description of what happened probably will be more interesting than the numbers. For example, "The first male stood up on his hind legs, wagging his tail like crazy. He walked up to the intruder and sniffed his nose, and all of a sudden they were rolling around and around. I couldn't tell who jumped on who!"

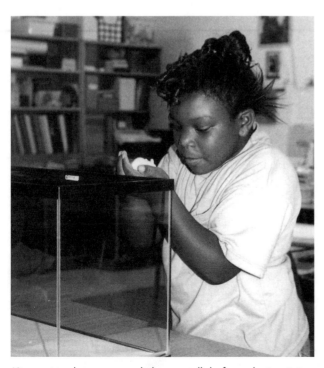

Kiara gives her mouse a little pep talk before placing it in the strange mouse's terrarium.

Conclusion

In the conclusion of this experiment, the children either accept or reject their own hypotheses. Then they try to make sense of their observations, to explain what they saw. Why did the male attack the intruder but the female did not? Are males always more aggressive? Or only toward intruders? Conclusions will be easier to draw after looking at this experiment together with the results of the next three experiments.

Identifying the Experimental Concepts

The **experimental variable** in this experiment is the sex of the resident mouse. We're looking at the effect of gender on the behavior of the resident toward the intruder.

The **control** here is the fact that we're examining the behavior of both genders. Each one controls for the other. If we looked only at the behavior of a male mouse against a male intruder, we couldn't attribute any of his behavior to his gender. But by trying the same thing with a female, we can. We can say that what caused the differences in their behavior must have been their gender.

The **dependent variable** is the mouse's reaction to the intruder. That reaction depends on the mouse's gender, apparently. In numerical terms, the dependent variable is the number of trials in which the male resident attacked the intruder, and the number of trials in which the female resident attacked the intruder.

The **controlled variables** are all the factors that were held constant, or that stayed the same, during all the trials. The cage was the same, as were the contents of the cage, the age of the mice (adult versus juvenile), the sex and age of the intruder, and so on. Since all these factors stayed the same, the only thing that varied was the gender of the resident mouse. So that's the only factor that could have caused the different outcomes.

The need for **multiple trials** in this experiment is met by introducing the intruder to the male three times (three trials) and to the female mouse three times (three trials).

Extension

Repeat the experiment using gerbils.

Extension

Repeat the experiment using hamsters. See the last section of the Introduction for a summary of the differences among mice, gerbils, and hamsters in the factors that provoke aggression.

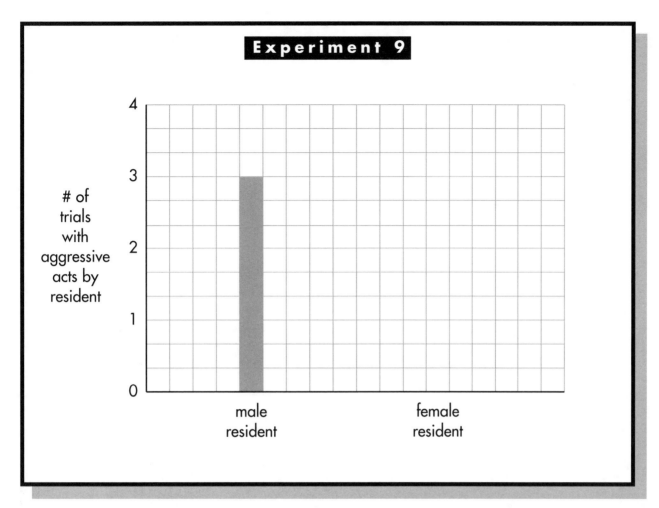

Experiment 9—One possible outcome of three trials introducing a male to a male, and three trials introducing a male to a female.

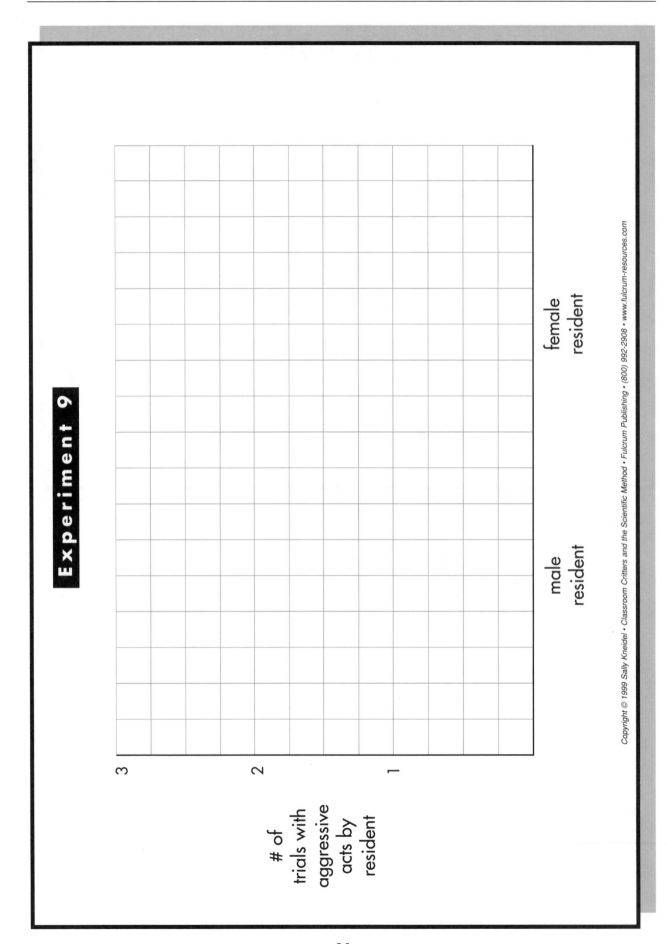

Experiment 9

# of trials with aggressive acts by resident

3

2

1

male resident

female resident

Copyright © 1999 Sally Kneidel • Classroom Critters and the Scientific Method • Fulcrum Publishing • (800) 992-2908 • www.fulcrum-resources.com

Name: _____

Experiment 9

Question: Are male mice and female mice equally aggressive toward male "intruders"?

Hypothesis: I think _____

_____

Materials: _____ _____

_____ _____

Procedure: We put a male mouse alone in a terrarium. After 10 minutes we put another male in with him. We recorded what happened. We repeated this procedure on two other days. Then we put a female mouse into a terrarium alone. After 10 minutes we introduced a male mouse. We recorded what happened. We repeated this procedure on two later days.

Results: Describe the behaviors seen in each trial:

	two males	a female and a male
Trial 1		
Trial 2		
Trial 3		
	Number of trials with agressive acts, for two males: _____	Number of trials with aggressive acts, for a male and a female: _____

Conclusion: _____

_____

_____

Copyright © 1999 Sally Kneidel • Classroom Critters and the Scientific Method • Fulcrum Publishing • (800) 992-2908 • www.fulcrum-resources.com

Experiment 10

Question

Does Aggression in a Male Mouse Depend Upon the Sex of the Intruder?

Hypothesis

I think male mice will be (a) more aggressive toward male intruders, (b) more aggressive toward female intruders, or (c) equally aggressive or nonaggressive toward both genders.

Materials

- at least one terrarium with a lid
- two or more adult male mice
- one or more adult female mice
- one piece of stiff cardboard at least 18 inches long and the same width as the terrarium
- food and a food container
- water and a water container
- litter or newspaper for the floor of the terrarium

Procedure

To begin the experiment, put the male mouse in the terrarium. Add food and water and some sort of nesting material if you plan to leave him in there longer than an hour. Give him at least 10 minutes to get used to the terrarium. Then lower a male into the terrarium, holding him by the tail. Remove your hand quickly. Observe and record what happens. If the mice fight, separate them with the piece of cardboard, keeping your hand

William and Jessica get acquainted with the mouse before starting the experiment.

on the other end of the cardboard 18 inches away. If they are fighting, they will probably bite your hand if you give them the opportunity. Keep the edge of the cardboard against the floor of the terrarium, separating them, for at least 5 minutes before attempting to remove the intruder. If he still appears upset, wear a heavy glove when picking him up. Repeat the entire procedure twice more, either using different mice or the same mice on different days, to be sure your mice are calm when beginning. Clean out the terrarium thoroughly between trials, because individual animals' scents can influence their behavior. You'll then have three trials in all. If you did Experiment 9, you can use the data from the three trials with two males instead of doing the above.

Now repeat the experimental procedure using an adult female mouse as the intruder (introducing a female to an already present male). You'll need to do three trials of this combination, too. Once again, use different individuals if possible, or do the trials on different days, so the mice can start fresh. Clean out the terrarium between trials.

Results

In my experience, two male mice will fight. The male resident will not fight the female intruder. As in Experiment 9, the children can record quick notes on the worksheet about observed behaviors, perhaps writing them out more fully later. For example, "When I put the female into the cage, the male just sniffed her stomach, and under her tail. She just stood there like she was scared. Then he ignored her." The children can also record on a worksheet the number of trials when a fight occurred, for each of the two gender combinations. That total will probably be three trials for the male intruder, and zero trials for the female intruder. But more interesting will be anecdotal information about what happened.

Conclusion

In the conclusion, the children either will accept or reject their own hypotheses. Then they will attempt to explain their results. Why did the male attack the male intruder but not the female intruder? How do these results fit together with the results of Experiment 9?

Identifying the Experimental Concepts

The **experimental variable** in this experiment is the sex of the intruder. In Experiment 9 the experimental variable was the sex of the resident.

The **control** here is the testing of both genders. We can compare the results for one gender with the results for the other in order to draw our conclusions. We can only comment on how maleness affected the male intruder's behavior, or his reception, if we have a nonmale intruder to look at as well, and vice versa.

The **dependent variable** is the reaction of the resident mouse. His reaction depends upon the sex of the intruder.

The **controlled variables** are all the factors that were kept the same, which included everything about the experimental setting (the terrarium) and the timing. Everything that could possibly have affected the resident's behavior was kept the same, except for the sex of the intruder. Thus we can say that any differ-ences in the resident's behavior must have been due to the sex of the intruder.

The need for **multiple trials** was met by doing three trials with two males and three trials with a male and a female.

Extension

Add one more set of trials, in which both the resident and the intruder are female. Compare it with the male-male trial. Your question could be something like, "Do two adult females behave differently than two adult males in a terrarium together?" Even though this question doesn't mention residents or intruders, you would still need to put one female in first, let her get used to it, then add the second. That's because your procedure would have to be the same as the male-male trials in order to compare them. Your experimental variable would be the gender of both resident and intruder.

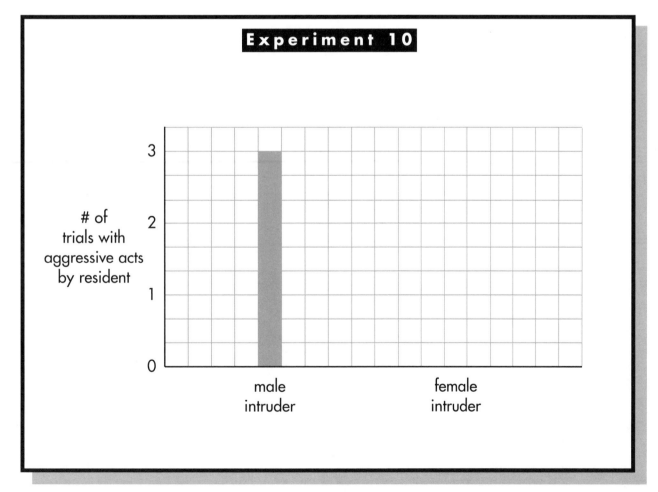

Experiment 10—One possible outcome of three trials introducing a male to a male, and three trials introducing a female to a male.

Extension

Repeat the experiment with gerbils, adding a set of three trials where both resident and intruder are female. Your experimental variable will be the gender of both resident and intruder. Or if you want to compare these results with the results in Experiments 9 and 10, the experimental variable will be species. The results will not be exactly the same as with mice.

Extension

Repeat the experiment with hamsters, adding a set of three trials where both resident and intruder are female. Your experimental variable will be the gender of both resident and intruder. Or if you want to compare these results with the results in Experiments 9 and 10, the experimental variable will be species. The results will not be exactly the same as with either mice or gerbils.

See the last section of the Introduction for a summary of the differences among mice, gerbils, and hamsters in factors that affect aggression.

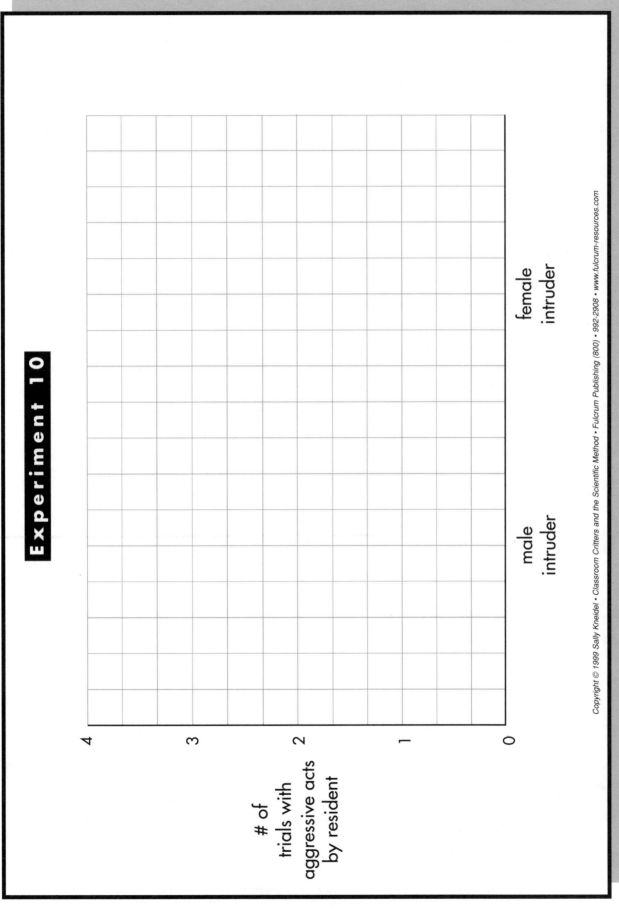

Experiment 10

# of trials with aggressive acts by resident

4

3

2

1

0

male intruder

female intruder

Copyright © 1999 Sally Kneidel • Classroom Critters and the Scientific Method • Fulcrum Publishing (800) • 992-2908 • www.fulcrum-resources.com

Name: _____

Experiment 10

Question: Does aggression in a male mouse depend upon the sex of the intruder?

Hypothesis: I think _____

_____

Materials: _____ _____

_____ _____

Procedure: We put a male mouse alone in a terrarium. After 10 minutes we put another male in with him. We recorded what happened. We repeated this procedure on two other days. Then we started over by putting another male mouse into a terrarium alone. This time, after 10 minutes we introduced a female mouse. We recorded what happened. We repeated this procedure on two later days.

Results: Describe the behaviors seen in each trial:

	two males	a female and a male
Trial 1	_____	_____
Trial 2	_____	_____
Trial 3	_____	_____

Number of trials with agressive acts, for two males: _____

Number of trials with aggressive acts, for a female and a male: _____

Conclusion: _____

_____

_____

Copyright © 1999 Sally Kneidel • Classroom Critters and the Scientific Method • Fulcrum Publishing • (800) 992-2908 • www.fulcrum-resources.com

Experiment 11

Question

Is a Male Gerbil More Aggressive Toward an Intruder That Is Familiar or One That Is Not Familiar?

Hypothesis

I think a male gerbil's aggression toward a familiar intruder will be more than / less than / the same as aggression toward an unfamiliar intruder.

Materials

- at least one terrarium with a secure lid
- three or more adult male gerbils, two of which are littermates and one of which is a stranger to the other two
- one piece of stiff cardboard at least 18 inches long and the same width as the terrarium
- food and a food container
- water and a water container
- litter or newspaper for the floor of the terrarium

Procedure

Put one of the littermates into the terrarium and give him at least 10 minutes to get used to his new surroundings. If you plan to have him in there for an hour or more, prepare the terrarium in advance with nesting material, food, and water.

Introduce another male, a littermate of the first one, into the terrarium. Record any behaviors you observe, including standing up, tail-lashing, sniffing, and stomping. If the gerbils fight, separate them right away by pressing the edge of the cardboard between them until it rests against the floor. Keep your hand on top of it, 18 inches away, so you won't get bitten.

Repeat this twice more, using different littermates, or on different days, so the gerbils will be calm when you start. Clean out the terrarium between trials to be sure no scents will affect their behavior.

To test the reaction to a nonfamiliar male, set up a male as before in the terrarium. After at least 10 minutes, lower another adult male gerbil into the terrarium with him, a male the original gerbil has not seen before. Record all the behaviors you observe. If they fight, press the edge of the cardboard between them right away, keeping your hand on the top edge of the cardboard.

Repeat this twice more, using different gerbils, or on different days, once again so the gerbils will start in a calm state.

Alexis and Lauren allow the mouse a short romp before getting down to business.

Results

The results are both the number of trials in which the gerbils fought, for each category (littermates or strangers), as well as any behaviors observed. Male gerbils that are littermates and have been living together generally will not fight. Male gerbils that are strangers generally will fight. So the number of trials where fights occurred, with littermates, will probably be zero. The number of trials where fights occurred with strangers will probably be three.

Conclusion

In writing up a conclusion, the children first accept or reject their hypotheses. Then they attempt to explain their results. The littermates don't fight because, in nature, gerbils live in a community of family members. They generally live peacefully with their relatives. This is not true of all rodents, so the outcome may be different with other species.

Identifying the Experimental Concepts

The **experimental variable** in this experiment is the familiarity or strangeness of the intruding gerbil. That's the only difference between the two sets of trials.

The **control** is the testing of both familiar and nonfamiliar intruders. We're able to draw a conclusion because we compare the two sets of trials with each other. Either alone would be meaningless. We can comment on the effect of an introduced male family member because we have observations of an introduced stranger to compare. A control just gives you something to compare your results to.

The **dependant variable** here is the reaction of the resident gerbil. His reaction depends upon the experimental variable—the familiarity of the intruding gerbil.

The **controlled variables** were all the factors that were kept the same, factors that could have affected the results. These include the contents of the terrarium, the presence of extra gerbils, the maturity of

the gerbils (juveniles react differently), any disturbances from outside the terrarium, such as loud noises or children's hands, and so on.

The need for **multiple trials** is met by doing three trials with littermates and three trials with strangers.

Extension

Try this experiment with mice. The results will not be the same, because mice do not live communally as adults. Adult males will fight whether they are littermates or not.

Extension

Try this experiment with hamsters. Males will fight whether they are littermates or not.

Extension

Try this with females. Female mice will not fight, regardless of familiarity. Female hamsters will fight, regardless of familiarity. Unfamiliar female gerbils will fight, but female littermates will not. These are generalities; there are individual exceptions to all.

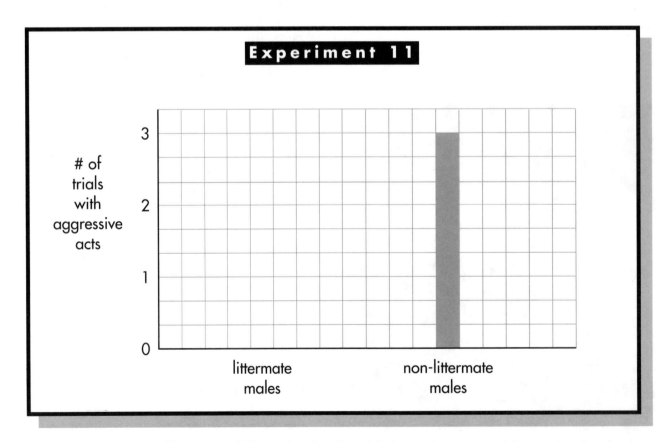

Experiment 11—One possible outcome of three trials with male gerbils that are littermates and three trials with male gerbils that are not littermates.

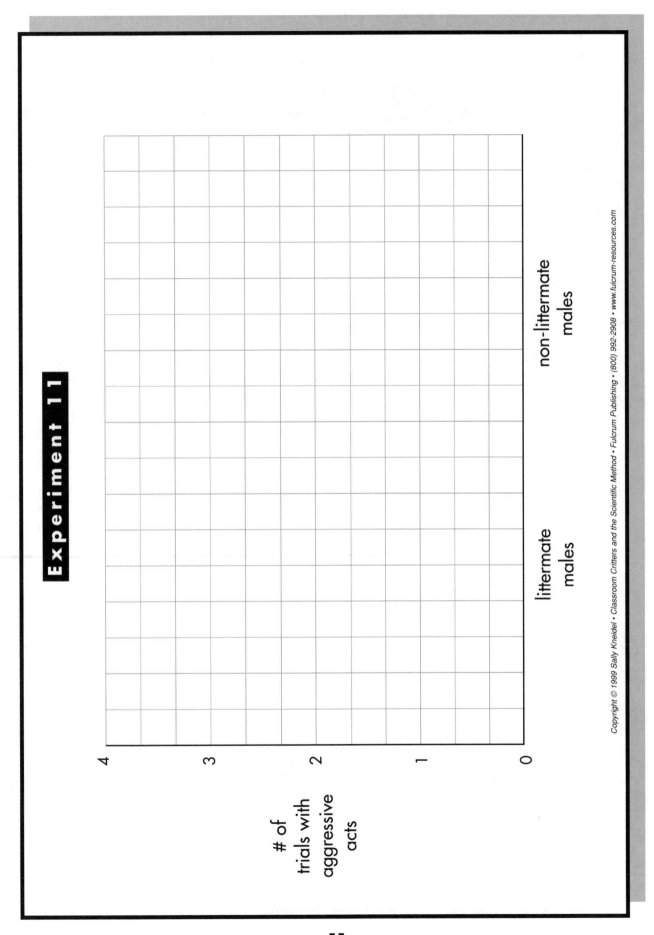

Experiment 11

# of trials with aggressive acts

0   1   2   3   4

littermate males   non-littermate males

Copyright © 1999 Sally Kneidel • Classroom Critters and the Scientific Method • Fulcrum Publishing • (800) 992-2908 • www.fulcrum-resources.com

Name: _____

Experiment 11

Question: Is a male gerbil more aggressive toward an intruder that is familiar or one that is not familiar?

Hypothesis: I think _____

_____

Materials: _____   _____

_____   _____

Procedure: We put an adult male gerbil alone in a terrarium. After 10 minutes we put in another male that was a littermate with him. We recorded what happened. We repeated this procedure on two other days, using different littermates. Then we started over, once again, with an adult male gerbil alone in a terrarium. This time we added a male gerbil that was a stranger, not a littermate. We recorded what happened. Then on two later days we repeated the procedure, again adding a strange male each time.

Results: Describe what happened in each trial.

	two littermate males	two non-littermate males
Trial 1		
Trial 2		
Trial 3		

Number of trials with agressive acts, for littermate males: _____   Number of trials with aggressive acts, for non-littermate males: _____

Conclusion: _____

_____

_____

Experiment 12

Question

Which Is More Aggressive—a Resident or an Intruder?

Hypothesis

I think the resident will be more aggressive than / less aggressive than / equally as aggressive as an intruder.

Materials

- at least one terrarium with a lid
- four to six adult male mice
- one piece of stiff cardboard at least 18 inches long and the same width as the terrarium
- food and a food container
- water and a water container
- litter or newspaper for the floor of the terrarium

Procedure

Set up the water, food, and floor covering (litter or newspaper). Individually mark each mouse to be used by putting a color on the back of his head, using a marker. Put one adult male mouse in the terrarium and leave him for at least an hour. Add a second adult male mouse, holding him by the tail. Observe and record what happens, particularly noting which one tends to dominate the other. If the mice fight, separate them with the piece of cardboard, keeping your hand on the other end of the cardboard 18 inches away. Repeat this experiment at least two more times, using in each trial at least one mouse that hasn't been used in this experiment before. The reason for this is that the outcome of a previous encounter between two mice (who won the last time) might affect the outcome of later encounters.

Results

In the "Results" section, the children record their observations. They also record, for each trial, which mouse seemed to dominate the other. If they want to, they also can count the number of particular behaviors, such as tail-lashing, in each situation. If they do, be sure they count for the same amount of time in each trial.

Conclusion

In the conclusion, the children either accept or reject their hypotheses. Then they attempt to

Chekeya and Joanne are intrigued as the mouse scampers from palm to palm.

explain their results. Was there any difference? If so, why? Does a resident mouse have more at stake (his home and territory) than an intruder does?

Identifying the Experimental Concepts

The **experimental variable** in this experiment is the status of the mouse as a resident or an intruder. We're comparing the behavior of residents and intruders.

The **control** here is having mice in two categories (resident and intruder) whose behavior we can compare. We need to make sure that the only difference between the two is their identity as resident or intruder.

The **dependent variable** here is the reaction of each mouse. We're hypothesizing that their reaction to the other mouse depends upon their position as resident or intruder. We're predicting that the resident mouse will be more aggressive.

The **controlled variables** are all the variables that could affect the behavior of each mouse, such as its sex, age, health, and hunger. All of these factors must be kept the same for the test mice.

The need for **multiple trials** is met by making observations over three trials.

Extension

Repeat the experiment with gerbils.

Extension

Repeat the experiment with hamsters. See the last section of the Introduction for a summary of the differences between hamsters, mice, and gerbils in the factors that affect aggression.

Name: _____

Experiment 12

Question: Which is more aggressive—a resident or an intruder?

Hypothesis: I think _____

_____

Materials:_____   _____

_____   _____

Procedure: We put one marked adult male mouse into a terrarium for one hour. Then we introduced a second adult male mouse. We observed and recorded what happened, particularly which dominated the other. Then we repeated this procedure _____ times, using in each trial at least one new adult male mouse.

Results: Describe what happened in each trial:

Trial 1 _____

Trial 2 _____

Trial 3 _____

Which one dominated, the resident or the intruder?

Trial 1 _____

Trial 2 _____

Trial 3 _____

Which mouse was more dominant overall?_____

Conclusion: _____

_____

Copyright © 1999 Sally Kneidel • Classroom Critters and the Scientific Method • Fulcrum Publishing • (800) 992-2908 • www.fulcrum-resources.com

Experiment 13

(Note: Experiments 13 and 14 should be done with gerbils. I don't know whether these experiments would work with mice or hamsters.)

Question

Are Gerbils Territorial? That Is, Do Adult Gerbils Living Together Use Different Portions of the Terrarium?

Hypothesis

I think the gerbils will use different / the same portions of the terrarium.

Materials

- a 20-gallon size terrarium (30 inches by 12 inches, 76 cm x 30 cm, or larger) with a lid
- two adult male gerbils and two adult female gerbils that have been living together in the terrarium for at least a week
- wood shavings to a depth of 2 inches (5 cm) on the floor
- two jars (roughly 1-pint or 1-pound size) inside the terrarium, for gerbils to rest in
- a sheet of clear transparent plastic such as Plexiglas (often available at picture framing shops), large enough to cover the top of the terrarium
- a grease pencil or other marker that will write on the Plexiglas
- a ruler or meter stick for making a grid

Procedure

These observations will be made in the gerbils' home terrarium. An ideal size would be about 36 inches x 24 inches (91cm x 61cm) in floor space. This would give the gerbils plenty of room to establish territories. But you probably would have to make one of wood and/or plexiglass, to have one this size. Otherwise, use the largest terrarium you can find.

All gerbils will be present during all observations, although only one gerbil's movement will be recorded during any one observation period.

For the purpose of recording gerbils' locations, make a grid on the Plexiglas lid of the terrarium, with squares 2 inches by 2 inches (5 cm x 5 cm). The grid should be the same size as the floor of the terrarium. Make a similar grid on a sheet of paper for recording results, and make copies of it. The paper grids can be smaller, but the number of squares and the shape must be the same as on the plexiglass lid. The children will watch the gerbils from overhead. Mark each gerbil on the back of the head with a marker or Wite-Out in such a way that the children can tell them apart. Each time the head of a gerbil enters a square on the plastic grid, a check is recorded on the paper grid. Observation periods of 15 minutes work well. With a class, you may want to do as many as 20 observations per gerbil. You may need that many to get reliable results. But if only one or two children are doing it, try fewer observations and see what happens. The gerbils will move quickly, so the children can just trace a line on the paper as the gerbils move around, and fill in the check marks later. It will be easier for the children to find the right squares on their papers

Brandon traces the movements of Gerbil A onto his paper grid.

if you number the plexiglass squares and put matching numbers on the paper grid.

Results

To map the overall territory of a particular gerbil, get a blank paper grid and shade or color each square that the gerbil entered during any and all of the observations. It doesn't matter whether the gerbil entered it once in one observation or ten times in every observation. If he or she entered the square at all, shade it. The total shaded area is the territory of that particular gerbil. Now repeat this procedure, using a fresh paper grid for each gerbil.

If you can, photocopy each territory on a clear transparency for an overhead projector. Then you can see how much the territories overlap by laying the transparencies over one another.

After you've shaded the squares for each gerbil, count how many squares you shaded for each one. Write this number on the worksheet (number of squares occupied over all observations) Then divide this number by the total number of squares on the grid (shaded and unshaded). This will tell you the percent of the terrarium floor used by that gerbil.

The results are the total number of shaded squares and the percents, one for each gerbil, and a filled-in paper grid for each gerbil, showing all the squares he or she crossed or occupied. Are the numbers the same? Are the filled-in grids, or territories, the same?

Conclusion

In the conclusion, the children either accept or reject their hypotheses. They also attempt to explain the results. Why are the numbers and the grids not the same for each gerbil? Gerbils are known to be territorial, even though they live communally, in family groups. Because they live in groups, their territories overlap quite a lot. However, the territories are not exactly the same. The territories of some are larger than those of others. The number of squares occupied by a particular gerbil reflects his or her social standing in the group. More dominant gerbils occupy larger territories.

These results have not actually demonstrated that gerbils are territorial or that the one who uses the most squares is dominant over the other. We've only shown that the number of squares occupied is not the same. We're either guessing about the reason, or trusting that other people's conclusions about gerbils are valid—that gerbils living together are territorial and that the more dominant ones have larger territories. Is there anything we can do that would further support this conclusion, that could make us more confident of our conclusion that the gerbil with the larger territory is dominant?

What if we could show that the gerbil with the larger territory dominates the other gerbil in every encounter? What if we could show that the one with the smaller territory retreats from every confrontation? That's what the next experiment is about.

Identifying the Experimental Concepts

The **experimental variable** here is really the relative dominance of the gerbils. We're predicting that the more dominant of the two gerbils will use more space, although that doesn't become clear until after Experiment 14.

This experiment doesn't really have a **control.** That's why it needs a follow-up experiment to verify our conclusions. A good control here would be to carry out the experiment with gerbils that are not territorial, so we could see whether they have a greater overlap in territory, which we would expect. But I don't think that's possible—I don't know of any gerbils that aren't territorial.

The **dependent variable** in this experiment is the number of squares entered by each gerbil.

The **controlled variables** are all the things that could affect the gerbils' movement but are not allowed to, such as children touching them or interfering in some way with one of the gerbils.

The need for **multiple trials** is met by doing up to twenty observation periods per gerbil.

Extension

Do the experiment separately with males and females. Are the differences in terrarium space usage among individual males greater than among individual females? Or are they the same, or less?

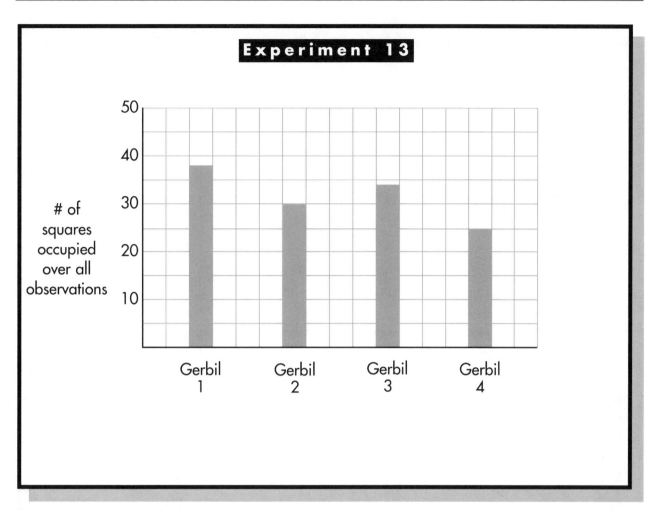

Experiment 13—One possible outcome, graphing the number of grid squares each gerbil entered at least once during any of the twenty observation periods.

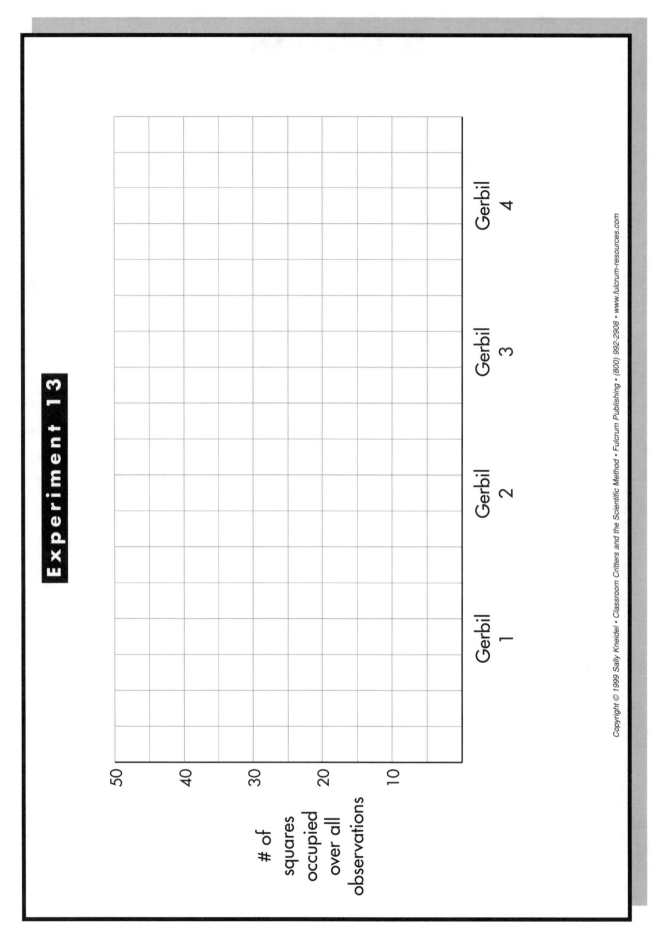

Experiment 13

# of squares occupied over all observations

50
40
30
20
10

Gerbil 1   Gerbil 2   Gerbil 3   Gerbil 4

Copyright © 1999 Sally Kneidel • Classroom Critters and the Scientific Method • Fulcrum Publishing • (800) 992-2908 • www.fulcrum-resources.com

Name: _____

Experiment 13

Question: Are gerbils territorial? That is, do adult gerbils living together use different portions of the terrarium?

Hypothesis: I think _____

_____

Materials:_____   _____

_____   _____

Procedure: We drew a 5 cm x 5 cm grid on a Plexiglas cover for our terrarium and a corresponding grid on several observation sheets (one per gerbil per observation period). We observed each adult gerbil for _____ observation periods. Each observation period lasted _____ minutes. During an observation period, each observer watched only one gerbil from overhead, marking on a paper grid each square entered by the gerbil being observed. After we finished the observations, we filled in for each gerbil a single grid sheet showing all the grid squares entered by that gerbil. We added the squares to get a total for each gerbil.

Results:

	# of squares occupied over all observations per gerbil	Percent of terrarium surface used per gerbil
Gerbil 1	_____	_____
Gerbil 2	_____	_____
Gerbil 3	_____	_____
Gerbil 4	_____	_____

Which gerbil occupied the most grid squares and the highest percentage of the terrarium surface?_____

Conclusion: _____

_____

Copyright © 1999 Sally Kneidel • Classroom Critters and the Scientific Method • Fulcrum Publishing • (800) 992-2908 • www.fulcrum-resources.com

Experiment 14

(Note: Experiments 13 and 14 should be done with gerbils. I don't know whether they would work with mice or hamsters.)

Question

Can We Predict, on the Basis of Past Behavior, Which Gerbil Will Back Away from a Confrontation in a Tunnel and Which One Won't?

Hypothesis

I think that a gerbil's reaction to a confrontation in a tunnel will be the same as his reaction at the last confrontation / will be the opposite of his reaction at the last confrontation / will vary, unrelated to his reaction to the last confrontation.

Materials

- two adult male gerbils and two adult female gerbils that live in the same terrarium
- a transparent plastic tube, approximately 3 inches in diameter (7–8 cm) and 9 to 12 inches long (23–30 cm), which can be purchased at pet stores.

Procedure

Place the tube in a secure place where it won't roll around. It should probably not be inside the terrarium, to eliminate the influence of any feelings of aggression or dominance that might be evoked by scents inside the terrarium. Mark the gerbils with a colored marker or Wite-Out on the top of their heads so that you can tell them apart. To test the gerbils, put two at a time into the openings at either end of the tube (one opening per gerbil). Record which one turns around and comes out first. Repeat this procedure nine times, for a total of ten trials per pair. Record each outcome. If there is no clear outcome after ten trials with each pair, do ten more trials per pair.

Results

With most pairs of gerbils, the same individual will turn around and come out first for all ten trials.

Virginia and Jonathan put two gerbils into the ends of the tunnel as Jack looks on.

Conclusion

In the conclusion, the children accept or reject their hypotheses, then try to explain the results they got. Why is the gerbils' behavior so consistent? Gerbils that have been living together have already established which of the two is dominant. When they encounter one another in the tube, they recognize each other, and behave according to their established relationship. The one that turns around and leaves is submissive. The one that holds his or her ground, refusing to budge, is dominant.

Identifying the Experimental Concepts

The **experimental variable** in this experiment is the social position of the gerbil. We're predicting that his social position relative to the other gerbil either will or won't influence its behavior.

The **control** in this instance is having animals with two different social positions. By choosing two adult gerbils that live together, we're ensuring that they do have different ranks. (In order to live together peacefully, they must have established a hierarchy.) We don't know which is which when we start, but we can assume that their ranks are different. Given that we already believe one is dominant and one is submissive, we're really asking whether the submissive one always turns around first when encountering a dominant animal. We're comparing the behavior of the submissive gerbil with the behavior of the dominant one.

The **dependent variable** is the gerbils' reaction to the encounter in the tube. Each individual's reaction depends on his social rank, relative to the other.

The **controlled variables** are those that are held the same during each trial. These possible influences are the location of the tube, absence of other gerbils, absence of distractions such as prodding fingers or shouts, health of the gerbils, and so on.

The need for **multiple trials** is met by doing ten tests of each pair of gerbils.

Extension

Try this experiment before doing Experiment 13. See if the results here enable the children to predict correctly the outcome of Experiment 14.

Extension

Try this experiment pairing adult gerbils with subadult gerbils. Does age have a predictable effect on outcome?

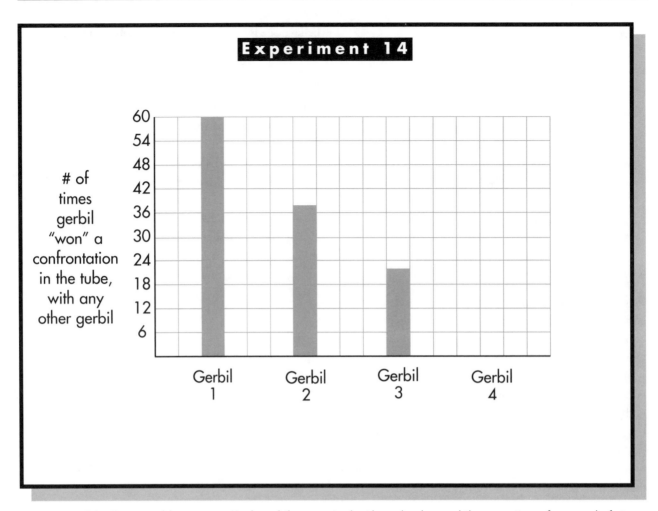

Experiment 14—One possible outcome. Each gerbil was paired with each other gerbil twenty times, for a total of sixty trials or pairings per gerbil.

Name: _____

Experiment 14

Question: Can we predict, on the basis of past behavior, which gerbil will back away from a confrontation in a tunnel and which one won't?

Hypothesis: I think _____

_____

Materials: _____ _____

_____ _____

Procedure: We tested two gerbils at a time, testing all possible pairs. A test (trial) consisted of introducing one gerbil of a given pair into each end of a transparent plastic tube. We recorded which one turned around and came out first. We repeated this procedure ten times with each pair of gerbils. (The first one out is submissive, the other is dominant.)

Results: Which came out first?

	Gerbils 1 & 2	Gerbils 1 & 3	Gerbils 1 & 4
Trial 1	_____	_____	_____
Trial 2	_____	_____	_____
Trial 3	_____	_____	_____
Trial 4	_____	_____	_____
Trial 5	_____	_____	_____
Trial 6	_____	_____	_____
Trial 7	_____	_____	_____
Trial 8	_____	_____	_____
Trial 9	_____	_____	_____
Trial 10	_____	_____	_____

Experiment 14 (continued)

Copyright © 1999 Sally Kneidel • Classroom Critters and the Scientific Method • Fulcrum Publishing • (800) 992-2908 • www.fulcrum-resources.com

Experiment 14 (continued)

	Gerbils 2 & 4	Gerbils 3 & 4	Gerbils 2 & 3
Trial 1	_____	_____	_____
Trial 2	_____	_____	_____
Trial 3	_____	_____	_____
Trial 4	_____	_____	_____
Trial 5	_____	_____	_____
Trial 6	_____	_____	_____
Trial 7	_____	_____	_____
Trial 8	_____	_____	_____
Trial 9	_____	_____	_____
Trial 10	_____	_____	_____

Record below, in the first two blanks for each pairing, which of the two gerbils emerged first most often and which emerged last most often.

	First	Last
Gerbils 1 & 2	_____	_____
Gerbils 1 & 3	_____	_____
Gerbils 1 & 4	_____	_____
Gerbils 2 & 4	_____	_____
Gerbils 3 & 4	_____	_____
Gerbils 2 & 3	_____	_____

Which one emerged first most often, overall?_____ Which one emerged last most often, overall? _____ Which one was most submissive? _____ Which one was most dominant? _____

Conclusion: _____

_____

_____

_____

Copyright © 1999 Sally Kneidel • Classroom Critters and the Scientific Method • Fulcrum Publishing • (800) 992-2908 • www.fulcrum-resources.com

Candace dips a cotton swab into "Scent D" as Whitney looks on and Kiara gets her data sheet ready to record the hamster's reaction.

Experiment 15

Question

Which Scents Cause a Reaction in a Hamster?

Hypothesis

I think hamsters will react to ammonia, fingernail polish remover, vinegar, and pickle juice.

Materials

- at least one hamster
- at least two cotton swabs for each substance tested
- several odorous substances to use for testing (very dilute ammonia, fingernail polish remover, vinegar, pickle juice, blue cheese, perfume, alcohol, turpentine, and any others)

Procedure

To test the hamster, dip one of the cotton swabs into one of the substances to be tested. Hold it to the hamster's nose, being careful not to touch his nose or his eyes. Record his reaction as either negative, positive, or no reaction. If a hamster doesn't like a smell, he may jerk his head away, perhaps violently. Or he may back away or turn around quickly. If he likes a smell, he may sniff at it repeatedly or try to take the swab. If he is indifferent, he will ignore the smell and continue to do whatever he was doing before you put the cotton swab near his nose. Test each substance at least three times, unless his reaction is unmistakable. Wait a minute or two between each test. As a control, hold a cotton swab that's wet with water in front of the hamster's nose. If you do three trials with each of the other scents, do three with water as well.

Results

Your results will be the number of reactions in each category (ignored, liked, disliked) for each substance tested. Results will include any other relevant behaviors observed.

Conclusion

In the conclusion, the children accept or reject their hypotheses, then try to explain the results they got. Did the hamster react the same way that people do to these smells? (To sniff ammonia, wave some air from over the ammonia toward your nose and take a quick, shallow sniff. Do not inhale deeply right over the container; it will painfully irritate your nose and breathing passages.)

Identifying the Experimental Concepts

The **experimental variable** in this experiment is the identity of the substance.

The **control** is testing the hamster with a plain wet cotton swab, which should not cause any reaction at all unless the hamster is very thirsty.

The **dependent variable** is the hamster's reaction to the various substances. His reaction depends upon which substance is on the cotton swab.

The **controlled variables** are those that are held the same during each trial. These include the location of the hamster, his surroundings, his freedom to move away from the cotton swab, the distance of the cotton swab from the hamster's nose, and the amount of substance on the cotton swab. Everything must be the same between trials except the identity of the substance being tested.

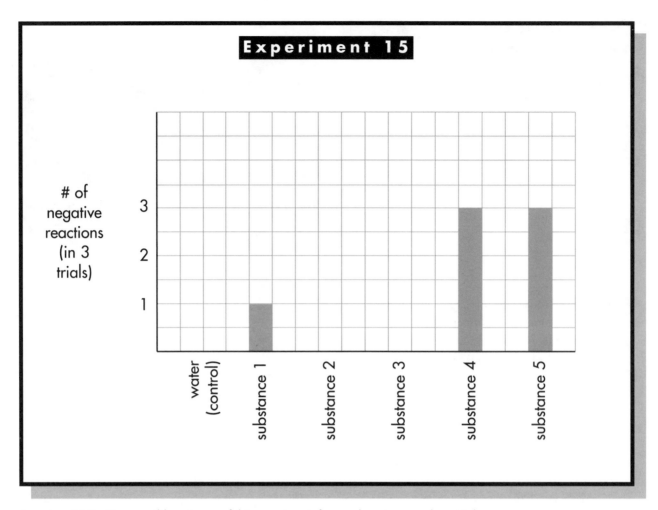

Experiment 15

of negative reactions (in 3 trials)

3

2

1

water (control)

substance 1

substance 2

substance 3

substance 4

substance 5

Experiment 15—One possible outcome of this experiment, for one hamster over three trials.

The need for **multiple trials** is met here by doing three trials with each substance.

Extension

Try the tests on different animals.

Extension

Try the tests on people, asking them to rate the smells as good, bad, or neutral. Tell your subjects to take a distant, shallow sniff if you use ammonia. A direct sniff can be painful.

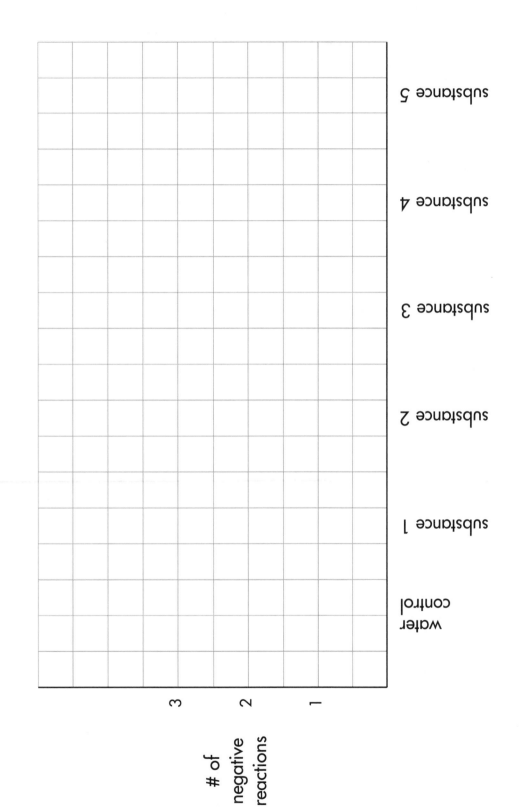

Experiment 15

# of negative reactions

3

2

1

water control

substance 1

substance 2

substance 3

substance 4

substance 5

Copyright © 1999 Sally Kneidel • Classroom Critters and the Scientific Method • Fulcrum Publishing • (800) 992-2908 • www.fulcrum-resources.com

Name: _____

Experiment 15

Question: Which scents cause a reaction in a hamster?

Hypothesis: I think _____

_____

Materials:_____ _____

_____ _____

Procedure: We collected several odorous substances. We tested our hamster with the substances one at a time. To begin, we dipped a clean cotton swab into one substance. We held the cotton swab under the hamster's nose, being careful not to touch his eyes or nose. Then we recorded the hamster's reaction.

Results: Record the hamster's reactions.

Substance	Trial 1	Trial 2	Trial 3	Overall, neg., pos., or no reaction
_____	_____	_____	_____	_____
_____	_____	_____	_____	_____
_____	_____	_____	_____	_____
_____	_____	_____	_____	_____
_____	_____	_____	_____	_____

Which substance did the hamster dislike? _____

Which substance did the hamster like? _____

Which substance did the hamster ignore? _____

Conclusion: _____

_____

_____

_____

Copyright © 1999 Sally Kneidel • Classroom Critters and the Scientific Method • Fulcrum Publishing • (800) 992-2908 • www.fulcrum-resources.com

Experiment 16

Question

Does the Scent of a Cat in a Terrarium Affect the Amount of Exploratory Behavior Displayed by a Gerbil?

Hypothesis

I think the scent of a cat in the terrarium will / will not affect the amount of exploratory behavior by a gerbil.

Materials

- a clean, relatively odorless terrarium
- bedding material, such as wood shavings, to cover the floor of the terrarium
- a sheet of clear Plexiglas to cover the top of the terrarium (also used in Experiment 13)
- a cat or access to a cat's used litter box
- 3 to 5 gerbils that live together or 3 to 5 mice that live together

Procedure

Mark the gerbils on the back of the head with Wite-Out or a marker so that you can tell them apart. Add wood shavings or shredded paper to the floor of a clean terrarium that is not the gerbils' home terrarium. Put in a few small items that the gerbils might explore, such as a small flowerpot on its side, a small box that opens to the side, and a short section of a paper towel roll. To provide a place where the gerbils might nestle down to sleep, settle some of the nesting material from their home terrarium in a cozy shape. Draw a grid on the Plexiglas with squares 2 inches x 2 inches (5 cm x 5 cm). Make a copy of the grid (it can be smaller) on a sheet of paper. To begin testing, introduce one gerbil to the terrarium, recording which gerbil it is. For 10 minutes, watch the gerbil by looking down on him through the Plexiglas grid. Every time he puts his head in a square, put a check in the same square on the paper. Numbering the squares beforehand, on both the Plexiglas and the paper, may help you keep track of which square is which. If the gerbil goes too fast to make checks, make a continuous line through the squares on the paper instead.

David works hard to trace the mouse's movements on the paper grid.

Now remove the gerbil. Replace him with gerbil number two and, on a fresh sheet of paper, put a check mark in every square his head enters for 10 minutes. Continue this procedure until all the gerbils have been tested, using a different sheet of paper for each gerbil.

After the last gerbil has been removed, put a cat into the terrarium. Attach a screen lid if necessary to keep it in there. You may have to give kitty a snack on a small plate to keep her happy. After 5 minutes, remove the cat and her snack. If the cat panics and won't stay for 5 minutes, you can sprinkle instead a small amount of used kitty litter into the terrarium.

Now repeat what you did with the gerbils above, once again marking every square that a gerbil's head enters.

Results

Add up the number of squares that got a check, for each gerbil, both before and after the cat. Compare each individual gerbil's "before cat" and "after cat" totals. How many gerbils moved around more before the cat odor was in the terrarium? Or did they move around more after the cat was in the terrarium? Or was there no difference? Now add the "before cat" totals and the "after cat" totals for all the gerbils so that you have one number for "before cat" and one number for "after cat." Which is higher? Is it a lot higher?

Conclusion

Here the children reject or accept their hypotheses, then try to explain their results. Why might the odor of a cat affect a rodent's behavior? Formal research has shown that mice, in areas where there are cat odors, hide in denser vegetation than in areas with no cat odors. With no vegetation present in the terrarium, the gerbil could spend more time holed up in his nest or in a box, hiding from the perceived cat. Or he could spend more time exploring, trying to find a way out of the terrarium. Or he may look around more at first, trying to escape, then give up and try to hide. Or it may be that gerbils don't react to cat odors, only mice do. In fact, not all mice do. Do hamsters? There are lots of possible outcomes here. Which did you predict?

Identifying the Experimental Concepts

The **experimental variable** here is the presence or absence of cat odors. We're predicting that the cat odors will affect the gerbil's behavior.

The **control** is testing the gerbil's activity in the absence of cat odors.

The **dependent variable** is the number of squares checked for the gerbil in the presence of cat odors. We're hypothesizing that any change in the gerbil's behavior depends upon the presence of cat odors.

The **controlled variables** are all the factors that could affect the outcome, such as any change in the terrarium other than the addition of cat odors, or any change in the subjects, such as drastic changes in the maturity of the animals, or using mice for the control and using gerbils after the cat odors were added.

The need for **multiple variables** here is met by using at least three animals for the control and at least three animals for the experimental portion (after the cat odors are added).

Extension

Do the addition of other, alternative odors affect the gerbils? What about the odor of a puppy? A snake? Another species of rodent? Do mice, hamsters, and gerbils react the same way to cat odors? Probably not.

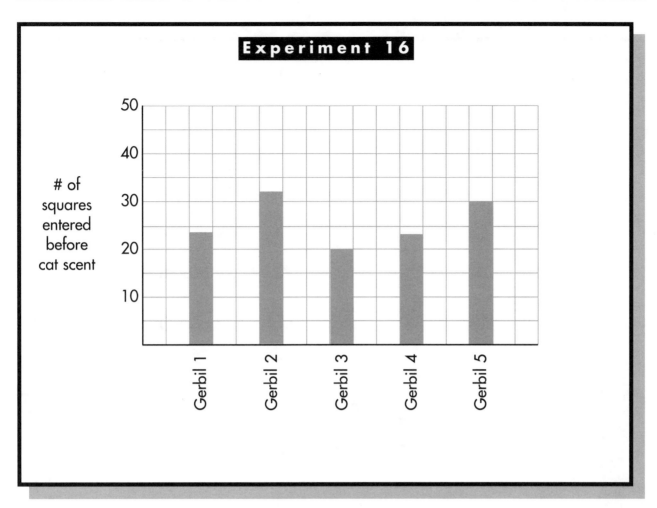

Experiment 16—The number of grid squares occupied per gerbil (each one alone) before cat scent is added to the terrarium. The graph shows one possible outcome of the "before cat" trials.

Experiment 16

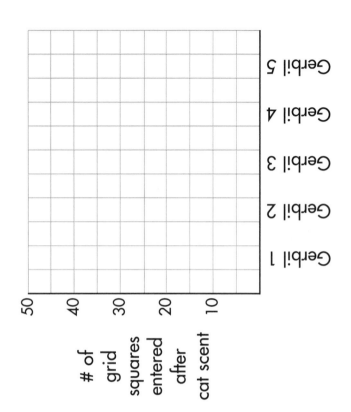

50 — 40 — 30 — 20 — 10

# of grid squares entered after cat scent

Gerbil 1 Gerbil 2 Gerbil 3 Gerbil 4 Gerbil 5

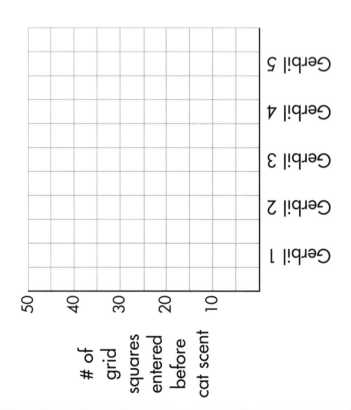

50 — 40 — 30 — 20 — 10

# of grid squares entered before cat scent

Gerbil 1 Gerbil 2 Gerbil 3 Gerbil 4 Gerbil 5

Copyright © 1999 Sally Kneidel • Classroom Critters and the Scientific Method • Fulcrum Publishing • (800) 992-2908 • www.fulcrum-resources.com

Name: _____

Experiment 16

Question: Does the scent of a cat in a terrarium affect the amount of exploratory behavior displayed by a gerbil?

Hypothesis: I think_____

_____

Materials:_____ _____

_____ _____

Procedure: We arranged a comforable test terrarium for the gerbils, different from their home terrarium. We drew a 2 inch by 2 inch (5 cm x 5 cm) grid on a piece of Plexiglas to place over the terrarium, and a comparable smaller grid on pieces of paper. We introduced a single gerbil into the terrarium and watched it from overhead for 10 minutes. Every time its head entered a grid square on the Plexiglas, we checked the corresponding grid square on a paper. Then we repeated this with _____(#) more individually marked gerbils, one at a time. Next we put a cat into the terrarium for 5 minutes. Then once again we mapped the movements of _____(#) gerbils, singly, on grid sheets. Finally, we added the number of grid squares entered by each gerbil before and after the cat.

Results: Record the number of grid squares entered by each gerbil.

	Gerbil 1	Gerbil 2	Gerbil 3	Gerbil 4	Gerbil 5	Total
Before cat in terrarium	_____	_____	_____	_____	_____	_____
After cat in terrarium	_____	_____	_____	_____	_____	_____

Conclusion: _____

_____

Copyright © 1999 Sally Kneidel • Classroom Critters and the Scientific Method • Fulcrum Publishing • (800) 992-2908 • www.fulcrum-resources.com

Experiment 17

Question

At What Age Do Mice Develop a Sensitivity to Odors? Which Odors Are They Sensitive To?

Hypothesis

I think the mice will first show a reaction to the odor at _____ days / weeks of age.

Materials

- at least one cotton swab for test
- water
- at least one odorous substance (vinegar, pefume, diluted ammonia)
- at least three newborn mice (called "pinkies")

Procedure

Test the baby mice every three or four days starting the day after birth until they are about three weeks old. Using at least three babies (for each substance) will give you a good idea of the degree of consistency between individuals. If you have seven test days, and you test three babies on each day, that's twenty-one tests. Three substances per test equals sixty-three times that a cotton swab is held to a mouse's nose—plenty for a whole class to do. You'll have to remove the mother to do the testing. Use a heavy leather glove or scoop her up with a cup. She'll probably try to bite you, to protect her babies. To test a baby mouse, separate the baby from its siblings and put it on a flat surface in front of your experimenter.

Here are the instructions for the child doing the testing. First, hold a cotton swab that's wet with water in front of the mouse's nose, as a control. Record the mouse's reaction on the worksheet provided. Then dip a dry cotton swab into an odorous substance to be tested. Hold the cotton swab to the mouse's nose, being careful not to touch its nose or eyes. If ammonia is being used, use a very dilute solution at first. If you get no reaction, gradually strengthen it and try again. Record the mouse's reaction to each substance. On the worksheet blanks, you might want to put + for a positive reaction, – for a negative reaction, and perhaps n.r. for no reaction. You also might write a few words to describe each reaction. These are words that might describe a negative reaction: twitches, pulls head back, moves arms as if to push away, flips over, moves away. A positive reaction might be sniffing repeatedly at the substance or trying to take the cotton swab. If a mouse is indifferent, it will ignore the substance and continue to do whatever it was doing before you put the cotton swab near its nose. If you're testing with more than one substance, wait a couple of minutes between tests, and do ammonia last. (Even very dilute ammonia may irritate its nose and affect its sense of smell for a while.)

Sara offers a scented cotton swab to a three-week-old gerbil.

The baby gerbil covers its nose in response to the smell.

Results

Results will be recorded on the worksheet. It might be useful for the children to summarize their overall findings in a paragraph on the back. Did the mice react to every smell? When they were newborns, were they able to react positively or only negatively? Did individuals react consistently? Do the children feel now that they could predict how any four-day-old mouse could react to a substance that was used in the tests? How did the mice's reactions change as they aged? Did they react differently to the odors than they did to the control (the water)?

Conclusion

In the conclusion, the children accept or reject their hypotheses, then try to explain the results. Why would it be adaptive for just-born mice to be able to react to foul odors? (An action is "adaptive" if it aids or could aid survival.) Why does their reaction change as they get older?

Identifying the Experimental Concepts

You could say that the **experimental variable** in this experiment is the age of the mice. We're asking how their age affects their reactions. But we're not actually manipulating their ages, we're just observing at different ages. The identity of the odorous substance might be a better experimental variable. In that case, we're really doing a separate experiment at each age.

The **control** here is the cotton swab with water on it. You do this to eliminate the possibility that the mice are reacting to the sight of a wet swab, rather than the odor.

The **dependent variable** is the reaction of the baby mice. Their reaction depends upon the identity of the substance (and their age).

The **controlled variables** are all those factors that could affect the outcome but are not allowed to, such as the species of rodent, the health of the babies, and the presence of other distracting stimuli.

The need for **multiple trials** is met by testing at least three baby mice.

Extension

By holding a nasty-smelling cotton swab to a baby mouse's nose daily for three weeks, could you teach the mouse to react negatively to the sight of a cotton swab? To answer this question, you could do just the experiment as described above, but using only the dilute solution of ammonia. As above, you would hold the swab briefly in front of the mouse's nose, allowing it to turn or move away and not touching the mouse with the swab. Ammonia is probably the most noxious smell you could use for a mouse. Record the mouse's reaction every day. On the last day, when it is three weeks old, you would hold in front of its nose a cotton swab that had been dipped only in water. Does the mouse begin to move away before you even get the swab near its nose, even though there is no ammonia on the swab? For a control, you could do the same thing with another cotton swab dipped in water and a second mouse that has never smelled anything unpleasant on a cotton swab. Does the second mouse react the way the first one does when it sees the swab coming?

Name: _____

Experiment 17

Question: At what age do mice develop a sensitivity to odors? Which odors are they sensitive to?

Hypothesis: I think _____

_____

Materials:_____ _____

_____ _____

Procedure: We tested three baby mice every _____ days for three weeks, starting the day after birth. To test a mouse, we dipped a cotton swab into a test substance and held it under the mouse's nose, not touching the mouse. We observed and recorded each mouse's reaction to each substance.

Results:

DAY 1

Substance	Mouse 1	Mouse 2	Mouse 3
water_____	_____	_____	_____
_____	_____	_____	_____
_____	_____	_____	_____
_____	_____	_____	_____
_____	_____	_____	_____
_____	_____	_____	_____
_____	_____	_____	_____

Experiment 17 (continued)

Copyright © 1999 Sally Kneidel • *Classroom Critters and the Scientific Method* • Fulcrum Publishing • (800) 992-2908 • www.fulcrum-resources.com

Experiment 17 (continued)

DAY 2

Substance	Mouse 1	Mouse 2	Mouse 3
water_____	_____	_____	_____
_____	_____	_____	_____
_____	_____	_____	_____
_____	_____	_____	_____
_____	_____	_____	_____
_____	_____	_____	_____
_____	_____	_____	_____

DAY 3

Substance	Mouse 1	Mouse 2	Mouse 3
water_____	_____	_____	_____
_____	_____	_____	_____
_____	_____	_____	_____
_____	_____	_____	_____
_____	_____	_____	_____
_____	_____	_____	_____
_____	_____	_____	_____

DAY 4

Substance	Mouse 1	Mouse 2	Mouse 3
water_____	_____	_____	_____
_____	_____	_____	_____
_____	_____	_____	_____

Experiment 17 (continued)

Copyright © 1999 Sally Kneidel • *Classroom Critters and the Scientific Method* • Fulcrum Publishing • (800) 992-2908 • www.fulcrum-resources.com

Experiment 17 (continued)

DAY 4

_____   _____   _____   _____

_____   _____   _____   _____

_____   _____   _____   _____

_____   _____   _____   _____

DAY 5

Substance	Mouse 1	Mouse 2	Mouse 3
water_____	_____	_____	_____
_____	_____	_____	_____
_____	_____	_____	_____
_____	_____	_____	_____
_____	_____	_____	_____
_____	_____	_____	_____
_____	_____	_____	_____

DAY 6

Substance	Mouse 1	Mouse 2	Mouse 3
water_____	_____	_____	_____
_____	_____	_____	_____
_____	_____	_____	_____
_____	_____	_____	_____
_____	_____	_____	_____
_____	_____	_____	_____
_____	_____	_____	_____

Experiment 17 (continued)

Copyright © 1999 Sally Kneidel • *Classroom Critters and the Scientific Method* • Fulcrum Publishing • (800) 992-2908 • www.fulcrum-resources.com

Experiment 17 (continued)

DAY 7

Substance	Mouse 1	Mouse 2	Mouse 3
water_____	_____	_____	_____
_____	_____	_____	_____
_____	_____	_____	_____
_____	_____	_____	_____
_____	_____	_____	_____
_____	_____	_____	_____
_____	_____	_____	_____

Did the reactions of the mice change as they aged? How?

Which substances did the mice dislike?

Which did they like?

Which were they indifferent to?

Conclusion: _____

_____

_____

_____

_____

_____

Copyright © 1999 Sally Kneidel • Classroom Critters and the Scientific Method • Fulcrum Publishing • (800) 992-2908 • www.fulcrum-resources.com

Experiment 18

Question

At What Age Do Mice Develop the Ability to Right Themselves When Flipped Over?

Hypothesis

I think mice will be able to right themselves at _____ days / weeks of age.

Materials

• at least three newborn mice

Procedure

This experiment requires testing at least three baby mice every two days starting the day of birth or the day after birth until they are all consistently able to right themselves. Using at least three babies will give you a good idea of the degree of consistency between individuals. Once again, you'll have to remove the mother to do the testing. Use a heavy leather glove or scoop her up with a cup. She'll probably try to bite, to protect her babies. To select a test mouse, separate one from its siblings and put it on a flat surface in front of the experimenter. The experimenter then gently turns the mouse onto its back (using his or her fingers), lets go of the mouse, and records the mouse's reaction.

Results

The results will be a report of the age of the mice when they were first able to right themselves.

Were they all the same age? Did they make efforts to right themselves on days before they did it successfully?

Conclusion

Here the children accept or reject their hypotheses. Why were the mice not able to right themselves at first? Can the children describe what muscle actions they lacked?

Identifying the Experimental Concepts

There is no **experimental variable** here, so this isn't truly an experiment. We're just observing developmental stages. We're not looking at the effect of some outside influence on the mice's ability to right themselves. In order to make this an experiment, we would need to ask how some outside factor affects their ability to right themselves. For example, you might ask, "Is a three-day-old mouse more likely to be able to right himself if he is in a fluffy nest than if he is on a flat, hard surface?" With that question, the experimental variable would be the nature of the surface. Or you might ask, "Is a three-day-old mouse more likely to right himself if it has littermates beside it?" With both of these above questions, your measurement could be the number of seconds required to flip over.

There is no **control** in the original design. But if you asked whether being in a fluffy nest helped the mice right themselves, then the control would be testing them as well on a flat, hard surface. In the "alone versus with littermates" version, the control would be testing a baby or babies in the absence of littermates.

At three weeks of age, the gerbil is able to right itself before the experimenter can remove her hand.

A baby gerbil at three weeks of age.

There is no **dependent variable** in the observation, but in the "fluffy nest versus hard surface" experiment, and in the "alone versus with littermates" experiment, the dependent variable is the number of seconds required for the mice to right themselves.

Controlled variables are irrelevant if you're not comparing two kinds of trials. In the original observations, you're not comparing any experimental setups. But in the experiment testing the effect of the surface and in the experiment testing the effect of the littermates, you would have to control any factor that could vary between the two situations being compared. You'd have to control the species of rodent, the age of the rodent, the amount of outside interference or distraction, and so on. These would be your controlled variables.

The need for **multiple trials** would be met by testing several different babies at each age level.

Extension

Do all the siblings in a litter develop the ability to right themselves at the same age?

Name: _____

Experiment 18

Question: At what age do mice develop the ability to right themselves when flipped over?

Hypothesis: I think _____

_____

Materials: _____ _____

_____ _____

Procedure: We tested the baby mice every other day, starting on the day of birth, until they were consistently able to right themselves. To test a mouse, we turned it onto its back and observed and recorded its response.

Results:

Day	Mouse 1	Mouse 2	Mouse 3
_____	_____	_____	_____
_____	_____	_____	_____
_____	_____	_____	_____
_____	_____	_____	_____
_____	_____	_____	_____
_____	_____	_____	_____

Conclusion: _____

_____

_____

_____

Copyright © 1999 Sally Kneidel • Classroom Critters and the Scientific Method • Fulcrum Publishing • (800) 992-2908 • www.fulcrum-resources.com

Experiment 19

Question

Does Mouse Development Follow the Same Sequence of Stages (Moving Limbs, Lifting Head, Creeping on Belly, Crawling on All Fours) That Human Development Does?

Hypothesis

I think mouse development will / will not follow the same sequence of stages as human development.

Materials

- at least three newborn mice

Procedure

This experiment involves testing three baby mice every two days starting the day of birth or the day after birth until they are all moving around as well as adults (around three weeks of age). Using at least three babies will give you a good idea of the degree of consistency between individuals. You'll have to remove the mother to do the testing. Use a heavy leather glove or scoop her up with a cup. She'll probably try to bite, to protect her babies. To test a baby mouse, separate one from its siblings and put it on a flat surface in front of the children who are observing. The baby will be uncomfortable in that situation and will be motivated to use all its muscle skills to get back to the nest. Write down everything you see the baby mouse do, for five minutes or so, until all its actions are repeats of actions you've already noted.

Results

The results will be a description of the behaviors you see at each age.

Conclusion

Here the children accept or reject their hypotheses. Did they see in the mice the same sequence of stages that humans follow in development? How closely related to humans are mice? The developmental stages of all mammals are very similar. In fact, the embryonic stages and developmental stages of most vertebrates are remarkably similar.

Identifying the Experimental Concepts

There is no **experimental variable** here, so this isn't really an experiment. We're just observing developmental stages, and comparing them with human developmental stages. To make this an experiment we would need to ask how some factor might affect the mice's developmental stages, or perhaps their rate of development. For example, we might ask, "Does the smallest mouse in a litter reach developmental milestones, such as lifting its head and creeping on its belly, on the same day as the larger mice in the litter?" With that question, the experimental variable would be the size of the mouse at birth or at the age of one day. Another question that would lead to an experiment is this: "Do mice from a large litter reach their developmental milestones on the same day as those from a small litter?" This question would only be interesting if we assume that mice in a large litter get less milk and hence grow more slowly. So we'd really be asking whether developmental rate depends upon growth rate. The experimental variable would be the size of the test mice's litters.

There is no **control** in the original design. But with the second question, the control would be the age at which developmental stages were reached by the larger mice. With the third question, the control would be the age at which developmental milestones are reached by mice in a smaller litter, who presumably get more milk.

There is no **dependent variable** in the observation. With the second question, regarding the runt of the litter, the dependent variable is the age at which various developmental milestones are reached. We're hypothesizing that this depends upon the size at birth. With the third question, regarding litter size, the dependent variable is also the age at which developmental milestones are reached.

In the original observation, you would need to **control** only those variables which might make the mice's development abnormal, since you're comparing their development stages with those of normal human development. You would want to make sure all the requirements for a normal development were met, such as providing water and food for the mother mouse, warmth, safety, nesting materials, and a calm environment. For the two experimental questions, regarding the runt and litter size, you'd have to control the species of rodent, the amount of outside interference or distraction, health of the mother, and so on. These would be your controlled variables.

The need for **multiple trials** would be met by observing several different babies for the original question, and also for both the control and the experimental trials of the second and third questions.

Extension

Have the children research the developmental stages of human babies, and if possible observe and compare the developmental stages of other mammals, such as a puppy or kitten, and some non-mammals such as a tadpole or caterpillar.

Name: _____

Experiment 19

Question: Does mouse development follow the same sequence of stages (moving limbs, lifting head, creeping on belly, crawling on all fours) that human development does?

Hypothesis: I think _____

_____

Materials:_____   _____

_____   _____

Procedure: We tested the baby mice every two days starting the day of birth or the day after. To test a mouse, we put it on a flat surface alone and observed and recorded all of its actions for 5 minutes.

Results:

Mouse 1

Day _____   _____

Day _____   _____

Day _____   _____

Day _____   _____

Day _____   _____

Day _____   _____

Day _____   _____

Day _____   _____

Day _____   _____

Day _____   _____

Day _____   _____

Experiment 19 (continued)

Copyright © 1999 Sally Kneidel • *Classroom Critters and the Scientific Method* • Fulcrum Publishing • (800) 992-2908 • www.fulcrum-resources.com

Experiment 19 (continued)

Mouse 2

Day _____ _____

Day _____ _____

Day _____ _____

Day _____ _____

Day _____ _____

Day _____ _____

Day _____ _____

Day _____ _____

Day _____ _____

Day _____ _____

Day _____ _____

Mouse 3

Day _____ _____

Day _____ _____

Day _____ _____

Day _____ _____

Day _____ _____

Day _____ _____

Day _____ _____

Day _____ _____

Day _____ _____

Day _____ _____

Day _____ _____

Conclusion: _____

_____

_____

_____

Copyright © 1999 Sally Kneidel • Classroom Critters and the Scientific Method • Fulcrum Publishing • (800) 992-2908 • www.fulcrum-resources.com

Experiment 20

Question

When Does the Ability to Rope-Climb Develop in Mice?

Hypothesis

I think the ability to rope climb develops at age _____ days / weeks.

Materials

- at least three newborn mice
- a stopwatch or clock with a second hand
- a length of cotton rope, 1/4 to 1/2 inch thick

Procedure

The children will need to test the three baby mice every two days starting the day of birth or the day after birth until they can turn around easily on the rope and climb down headfirst (around three weeks of age). Using at least three babies will give a good idea of the degree of consistency between individuals. To prepare for testing, attach the cotton rope to something so that it hangs vertically for several inches. Underneath it, place a soft surface to cushion the baby mice that fall from the rope. To get a baby mouse for testing, you'll probably have to remove the mother first. Use a heavy leather glove, or scoop her up with a cup. She'll probably try to bite, to protect her babies.

For the experimenter: Once you have a baby in hand for testing, hold it up to the rope so that all four of its feet are touching it. Support the baby like that for a few seconds, then let go. Record whether it falls. If it doesn't fall right away, record which feet actually attach to the rope and how many seconds the baby remains attached. Record whether it freezes in place or makes an attempt to turn around or to climb down. Write down any details you notice.

Mother gerbils seem to be more willing than mother mice to part with their youngsters temporarily. However, in my experience, young gerbils are not as adept as young mice at rope climbing.

Results

The results will be a description of the behaviors you see at each age, for each of the three mice. At what age were they able to hold on, without moving? At what age were they able to hold on with all four feet? At what age were they able to climb down backward or sideways? At what age were they able to turn around and climb down headfirst? Were the stages of success the same for the three individuals?

Conclusion

Here you accept of reject your hypothesis. You also attempt to explain it. Why do you think the three mice were so similar in the order in which the skills developed?

Identifying the Experimental Concepts

As in Experiments 18 and 19, there is no **experimental variable** here, so this isn't really an experiment.

Alan holds the three-week-old gerbil to the rope, which is suspended from a stick with a clothespin. The stick rests atop and between the backs of two chairs.

We're just observing developmental stages. To make this an experiment, we would need to ask how some factor might affect their rope-climbing success, some factor that we could manipulate or alter. We are asking how age affects it, but that's not a factor we can manipulate. For example, we might ask, "Can a fifteen-day-old mouse climb a nylon rope as well as it can a cotton rope?" With that question, the experimental variable would be texture of the rope. Another possibility would be asking, "Can a fifteen-day-old mouse climb a 1/8-inch-diameter rope as well as a 1-inch-diameter rope?" The experimental variable would be, for one, the texture of the rope, and for the other, the width of the rope.

There is no **control** in the original design. But with the second question, the control would be testing the mice on the cotton rope. With the third question, the control would be testing the mice with the 1-inch rope.

There is no **dependent variable** in the observation. With the second question, regarding rope texture, the dependent variable is the average number of seconds the mice hang onto each type of rope. We're hypothesizing that this depends upon the texture of the rope. With the third question, regarding rope diameter, the dependent variable is the average number of seconds the mice hang onto each diameter of rope.

In the original observation, there would be no **controlled variables**. For the two experimental questions, regarding the rope texture and rope diameter, you'd have to control the species of rodent, the amount of outside interference or distraction, age and health of the mice, and so on. These would be your controlled variables.

The need for **multiple trials** would be met by observing several different babies for the original question, and also for both the control and the experimental trials of the second and third questions.

Sara holds the three-week-old gerbil to the rope, which is suspended from a stick with a clothespin. The stick rests atop and between the backs of two chairs.

Name: _____

Experiment 20

Question: When does the ability to rope-climb develop in mice?

Hypothesis: I think _____

_____

Materials:_____   _____

_____   _____

Procedure: We tested three baby mice every ___ days, starting when they were ___ days old. We continued until they were ___ days old. To test a baby mouse, we held it up to a vertical rope and let go. We recorded whether it fell right away, hung on without moving (with one or more feet), backed down, or turned around and climbed down.

Results:

Day	Mouse A	Mouse B	Mouse C
____	_____	_____	_____
____	_____	_____	_____
____	_____	_____	_____
____	_____	_____	_____
____	_____	_____	_____
____	_____	_____	_____
____	_____	_____	_____
____	_____	_____	_____
____	_____	_____	_____
____	_____	_____	_____

Conclusion: _____

_____

Copyright © 1999 Sally Kneidel • Classroom Critters and the Scientific Method • Fulcrum Publishing • (800) 992-2908 • www.fulcrum-resources.com

CHAPTER 2

Goldfish and Guppies

Experiment 21

Question
Do Goldfish Hide?

Hypothesis
I think the goldfish will spend most of their time in the covered area / the well-lit area / both areas equally.

Materials
- goldfish (can be purchased more cheaply as "feeder fish," which are intended as food for larger fish or snakes)
- goldfish containers
  (*Note: I use clear plastic rectangular dishes for the goldfish, about 8 inches by 6 inches by 3 inches deep [20 cm x 15 cm x 7.5 cm deep]. The deli at the local grocery store donates them to me when I explain what I want them for, or sells them to me for 15 cents apiece. But a large aquarium would work, too.*)
- water
  (*Note: I use spring water from the grocery; pond water; or tap water that has had drops from a pet store added to remove chlorine or has been allowed to sit in a wide-open container for forty-eight hours—the chlorine will evaporate.*)
- a partial cover for the container
  (*Note: To create shade, I use a piece of black construction paper big enough to cover one side of the*

container and stick out a few inches beyond, so that it blocks some of the light coming from the sides as well. Laminating the black paper keeps it from bleeding into the water quite as fast if a student accidently knocks it in.)
- a piece of white paper at least as big as the aquarium, with a black line drawn through the middle, along the shorter axis (across the width, not the length of the paper)
- one clock with a second hand

Procedure
In a classroom setting, this works well with groups of four. Place each dish on a piece of white paper. On the paper is a black line you've already drawn, visible through the dish, which separates the shaded half of the dish from the other half. A line makes it easier for students to decide whether

Lauren tallies the goldfish's position. This time it's out from under the cover.

the fish is considered to be in the shade when it's time to make a tally mark.

Cover half of each dish with the laminated black construction paper.

Make sure the temperature of the water in the dishes is the same as in the fish's holding tank before moving the fish. Give them a minute or two to get used to the new container. Then have the children record the fish's position at 30-second intervals. If your fish are very active, shorter intervals might work. Longer intervals will certainly work if your students' attention spans can handle the waiting. Record observations for 10 minutes or so, or until you have at least twenty per group of children.

Disturbance tends to send the goldfish into the shade, so children should be cautioned against thumping the desk or the dish, or waving their hands and pencils around.

Results

Your results are a statement of the number of observations of fish in the shade and on the other side. The goldfish do tend to stay in the shade.

Conclusion

In the conclusion, each child either accepts or rejects his or her own hypothesis, thereby answering the original question. The children also attempt to explain the results. Why might an attraction to shade or cover have survival value for goldfish, or any fish? (They are not as visible to larger predatory fish.)

Identifying the Experimental Concepts

We're asking about the effect of shade on the goldfish's choice of location. So the **experimental variable** here is the amount of shade in the two halves of the tank.

Since we're asking about the effect of cover or shade, we must offer the goldfish an alternative to shade that is, in other respects, just the same. That alternative, the unshaded half of the container, is the control. The **control** enables us to say that any choice the goldfish makes is due to differences in shading.

The **dependent variable** is the goldfish's choice of location—the number of observations in each place.

The **controlled variables** are the type of water, water temperature, amount of disturbance, type of container, time of day, and so on. In this set-up, everything is the same between the two halves except the presence or absence of shade. Everything else that might affect the fish's movement is controlled; that is, not allowed to vary.

The **multiple trials** here are the several fish and the several containers. Or if you have only one fish, you can create multiple trials by repeating the procedure several times.

Extension

Natural ponds have shaded areas created by overhanging land forms or trees, or by sunken objects. Aquatic plants create another sort of shaded area or hiding place. The children may want to test whether goldfish will choose an area dense with underwater plants as an alternative to open water.

Elodea and hornwort are two plants that stay suspended in water without sinking or floating. Both are available at pet stores. In shallow water, these plants can be arranged on one side only so that they stay put. Again, a black line underneath the midline of the aquarium will help students make quick decisions about which side is which for tallying. For deeper water, you can make a partition of chicken wire for the center of the aquarium, which will keep plants on one side but will allow goldfish to pass freely.

Here the experimental variable is the presence of plants. The control is the area without plants. The dependent variable is the number of goldfish in each location.

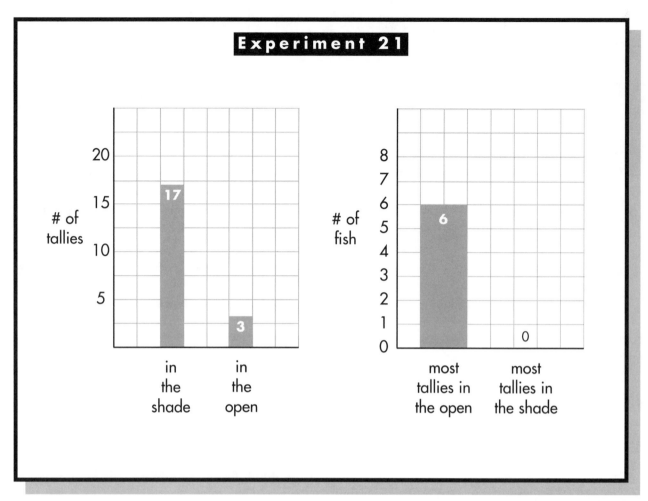

Experiment 21—The graph on the left shows one possible outcome for a single fish, with a tally every 30 seconds for 10 minutes. The graph on the right shows one way to graph class data. It shows the number of fish that spent most of their time (had most of their tallies) in the open.

Name: _____

Experiment 21

Question: Do goldfish hide?

Hypothesis: I think _____

_____

Materials: _____   _____

_____   _____

Methods: We placed a black sheet of paper over one half of the goldfish's container. We tallied the fish's position every _____ seconds for _____ minutes.

Results:

fish in the shade	fish in the open

total   class   total   class
tallies _____   total _____   tallies _____   total _____

Conclusion: _____

_____

_____

_____

Copyright © 1999 Sally Kneidel • *Classroom Critters and the Scientific Method* • Fulcrum Publishing • (800) 992-2908 • www.fulcrum-resources.com

Experiment 22

Question

What Is the Effect of Chilling on the Breathing Rate of Goldfish?

Hypothesis

I think chilling will increase / decrease / not affect the breathing rate of goldfish.

Materials

- one or more goldfish
- one cup per goldfish
- ice
- one plastic dishwashing tub for every ten goldfish cups, to hold an ice bath
- dechlorinated water
- one thermometer
- one clock

Procedure

This experiment works well with children working in pairs, each pair with one fish and one cup. It does require at least two people, even for children doing it at home. The overall idea is to count the number of fish respirations per minute at room temperature, then to chill the fish briefly by submerging the fish's cups in an ice bath, then count the number of fish respirations per minute again. Jelly glasses work very well to hold the fish. They are big enough to accommodate the length of an average goldfish, but small enough to restrict the fish's movement, which is a big help in counting the breaths. I buy feeder goldfish from a pet store. Specify that you want feeder fish,

William concentrates on counting the breaths of the goldfish in the jelly glass.

because they're much cheaper than pet fish, although they may look identical. Feeder fish are normally sold as food for larger fish or pet snakes.

When I do this experiment with a class, I set the fish in their glasses in advance. I fill the glasses about two-thirds full with water from the pet store or from the fish's aquarium. If this isn't possible, use bottled spring water (not distilled water) or water that has had dechlorinating drops added. Use a premoistened fish net or premoistened hands to transfer the fish to the glasses.

Fill two plastic tubs with ice, deep enough to cover most of the height of the glasses. But no deeper! A mixture of ice and water will do.

Describe to the children how to count fish respirations. When fish breathe, the mouth gapes open to take in water, then it closes. The water passes over the gills, then exits through the two slits on the fish's sides. These openings are covered by a flap called the operculum. You can see the operculum move somewhat as a gulp of water passes out. Children can count breaths by counting the number of times the mouth opens, which you can see most easily by looking through the glass. Or they can count the number of times the two opercula open, which can be seen by looking down on the fish from above or by looking through the glass. Have them practice counting before starting the experiment.

If you have enough thermometers to go around, let each pair of children take the temperature of the water in their cup before beginning. Caution them not to touch the fish or tap on the glass with the thermometer. If you have only one thermometer, have one person take the temperature of the water in one cup; they should all be the same. (Tell the children that clasping the glass with one or both hands will warm the water.) Everyone should record the starting temperature on the data sheet.

Children often make mistakes in counting the number of breaths in one minute. To compensate for this, at each temperature I have each pair of children do three trials and throw out the one that is most different from the other two. I ask them to average the remaining two. This average is their official count for that temperature. They do the same thing to arrive at a usable count for the other temperature as well.

Results

If you have only one fish, your results will be a statement of the number of fish breaths per minute, for room-temperature water and for cold water. If you have a class and several fish, each work group records their own counts on the data sheet. It's interesting then to take a total or average over the whole class.

Conclusion

Were the children's hypotheses correct or not? Have them try to explain their results in the conclusion. Why might a fish breathe more slowly in cold water? Fish are cold-blooded, or poikilothermic, meaning their body temperature depends on the temperature of the environment around them. When an animal's body temperature drops, its metabolism slows and all bodily processes slow. This includes heart rate, rate of digestion, and breathing rate. All cold-blooded animals breathe more slowly when chilled.

Identifying the Experimental Concepts

The **experimental variable** here is the temperature of the water.

The **control** is testing the fish in water at room temperature.

The **dependent variable** is the number of breaths the fish took, which we're hypothesizing is dependent on the water temperature.

The **controlled variables** are any factors that could influence the outcome but which are held constant between the two sets of trials, such as the size of the container, the type of fish, and the skill level of the people counting the breaths.

The need for **multiple trials** is met by having three trials at each temperature.

Joanne and Alex measure the temperature of the water in the goldfish's glasses. The glasses are partially submerged in an ice bath.

Extension

See if this experiment works with other animals. If you have access to a toad, frog, lizard, or snake, you can chill or warm him very slightly, no more than a 10 degree Fahrenheit change. Perhaps you could move the animal from an air-conditioned room to an 85 degree room. (Don't put him anywhere that would be very uncomfortable to a human.) Count his breaths per minute in the first room, then move him and give him 30 minutes for his body temperature to change. Then count his breaths per minute again.

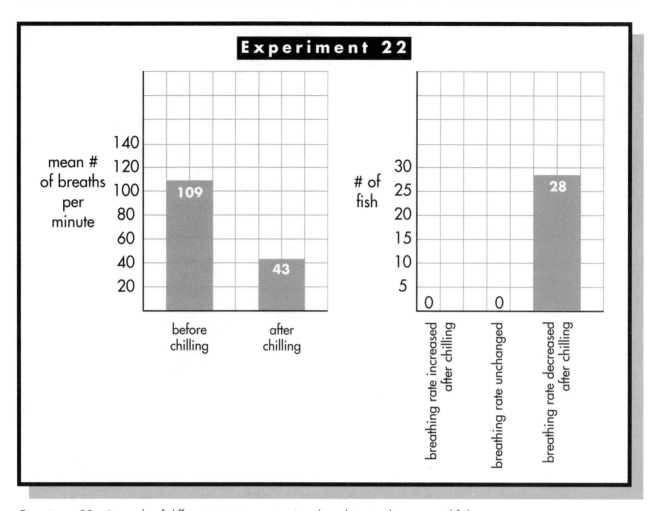

Experiment 22—A couple of different ways to summarize class data involving several fish.

Name: _____

Experiment 22

Question: What is the effect of chilling on the breathing rate of goldfish?

Hypothesis: I think _____

_____

Materials:_____   _____

_____   _____

Procedure: We put each test fish into a cup of room-temperature (_____°C) aquarium water. We counted the number of breaths per minute for each fish. Then we put ice around the cups until the water in the cups was about 10°C. We counted the number of breaths per fish again.

Results:

Number of breaths per minute
for **warm** fish   _____

Number of breaths per minute
for **cold** fish   _____

Class
average or total: _____

Class
average or total: _____

Conclusion: _____

_____

_____

_____

_____

_____

Copyright 1999 © Sally Kneidel • Classroom Critters and the Scientific Method • Fulcrum Publishing • (800) 992-2908 • www.fulcrum-resources.com

Experiment 23

Question

What Is the Effect of Chilling on the Rate of Movement of Goldfish?

Hypothesis

I think chilling will increase / decrease / not affect the rate of movement of goldfish.

Materials

- one or more goldfish
- one small aquarium or other container per goldfish
- ice
- one plastic dishwashing tub
- dechlorinated water
- one thermometer
- one clock

Procedure

I buy feeder goldfish from a pet store. Specify that you want feeder fish, because they're much cheaper than pet fish, although they may look identical. Feeder fish are normally sold as food for larger fish or pet snakes.

You will need, for each fish, a container big enough to allow some movement, perhaps a minimum of 4 inches by 6 inches (10 cm x 15 cm). Make a grid on a piece of paper with squares about 2 inches by 2 inches (5cm x 5cm). You may want to number the squares to avoid getting them mixed up. The entire grid size should match the size of the aquarium floor. Keep one copy of the grid handy for collecting data. Put another copy of the grid under the aquarium, so you can see it from above. If your aquarium has an opaque floor, you can make a grid on a clear sheet of Plexiglas instead, and put it over the aquarium.

Add dechlorinated water to the aquarium, ideally water from the fish's home aquarium. Put the goldfish in, making sure the temperature of the water is the same as the water he came from, and approximately room temperature. Use a pre-moistened fish net or premoistened hands to transfer the fish to the glasses.

Watch the fish for 5 minutes, checking a square on the grid every time the fish's head enters that square. If that's too challenging, just trace his path with a pencil, filling in the checks later. A child working alone or a class with only three fish should repeat this procedure at least twice more, with new data sheets and ideally with two different goldfish. You'll then have three 5-minute trials at room temperature.

The next step is to chill the fish, his aquarium, and his water by submerging the aquarium in an ice bath. Keep a thermometer in the fish's water. When the temperature gets to 10 degrees centigrade, remove the aquarium from the ice bath and once again trace the fish's path for 5 minutes. You'll need two more trials in cold water. Chilling and warming, chilling and warming a single fish in one day may kill him, so use different goldfish or do the other two cold trials on two different days.

If you have a class and a large number of fish, of course more replicates are always better.

Results

Your results will be a statement of how many squares the fish entered in each trial.

Conclusion

Were the children's hypotheses correct or not? Have them try to explain their results in the conclusion. Why might a fish move more slowly in cold water? Fish are cold-blooded, or poikilothermic, meaning that their body temperature depends upon the temperature of the environment around them. When a

Kiara and Virginia trace the movements of the goldfish on their papers, which are duplicates of the paper under the aquarium.

cold-blooded animal's body temperature drops, its metabolism slows, and all of its bodily processes slow, including breathing rate and rate of movement.

Identifying the Experimental Concepts

The **experimental variable** here was the temperature of the water.

The **control** was testing the fish in water at room temperature.

The **dependent variable** was the number of squares the fish entered, which we're hypothesizing is dependent on the water temperature.

The **controlled variable**s are any factors which could influence the outcome but that are held constant between the two sets of trials, such as the size of the container, number of fish in the container, and size of the grid squares.

The need for **multiple trials** is met by having three trials at each temperature.

Extension

Test the effect of temperature on movement of an insect—insects are also cold-blooded. Make a grid for the insect in a small terrarium. Test its rate of movement as you did for the fish here, then put the insect in a jar and chill the bug and the jar in the fridge for half an hour or in the freezer for about 2 minutes. Test the insect's rate of movement again.

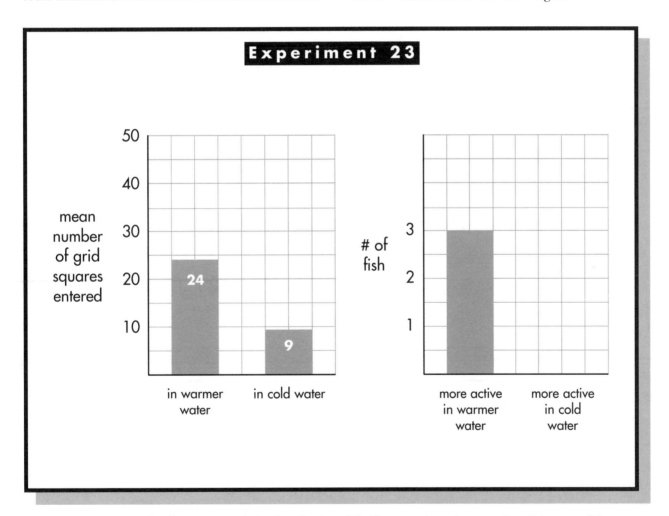

Experiment 23—A couple of ways to graph the data for three fish. The second graph means that all three test fish were more active in warmer water than in cold water.

Name: _____

Experiment 23

Question: What is the effect of chilling on the rate of movement of goldfish?

Hypothesis: I think _____

_____

Materials: _____ _____

_____ _____

Procedure: We put the test fish in a small aquarium, _____inches by _____ inches. We made a grid to go over or under the aquarium, and copies of the grid for recording data. Then we watched the fish for 5 minutes in warm (room-temperature) water. Each time the fish's head entered a grid square, we checked that square on our data sheet. Next we chilled the fish's water by putting ice around the aquarium. When the water was 10°C, we recorded the fish's movement across grid squares again for 5 minutes. We repeated the procedure with two other fish.

   Then we added the total number of grid squares entered in warm water to compare with the total number of grid squares entered in cold water.

Results:

	Number of grid squares entered in warm water	Number of grid squares entered in cold water
Fish A	_____	_____
Fish B	_____	_____
Fish C	_____	_____
	Total: _____	Total: _____
	Class total: _____	Class total: _____

Conclusion: _____

_____

Copyright © 1999 Sally Kneidel • Classroom Critters and the Scientific Method • Fulcrum Publishing • (800) 992-2908 • www.fulcrum-resources.com

Experiment 24

Question

Do Goldfish Eat Fewer Guppies When There Is Elodea Throughout the Aquarium?

Hypothesis

I think goldfish will / will not eat fewer guppies when there is elodea throughout the aquarium.

Materials

- six aquariums (or fewer if you use them in sequence)
- 120 guppies (newborns if your goldfish is less than 2.5 or 3 inches)
- six goldfish or twelve goldfish, all approximately the same size
- some sort of aquatic plant, such as elodea or hornwort, that will not float or sink, but will remain suspended in the water column in the aquarium

Procedure

Fill each of the six aquariums with water. Add drops from the pet store to dechlorinate it. Purchase at a pet store, or remove from a pond, enough elodea or hornwort to more or less fill three (and only three) of the aquariums. Leave the other three with no plants. There should still be room enough for the guppies to swim freely among the plants.

Introduce twenty guppies to each of the six aquariums. Allow them to get acquainted with the aquariums for an hour or so. Add either one or two goldfish to each aquarium. Be consistent—either one for each aquarium or two for each aquarium. If you can't find goldfish big enough to eat adult guppies (a 2 inch goldfish is not big enough), then you need to use guppies that have just been born. Even a 1.5 to 2-inch goldfish can eat newborn guppies.

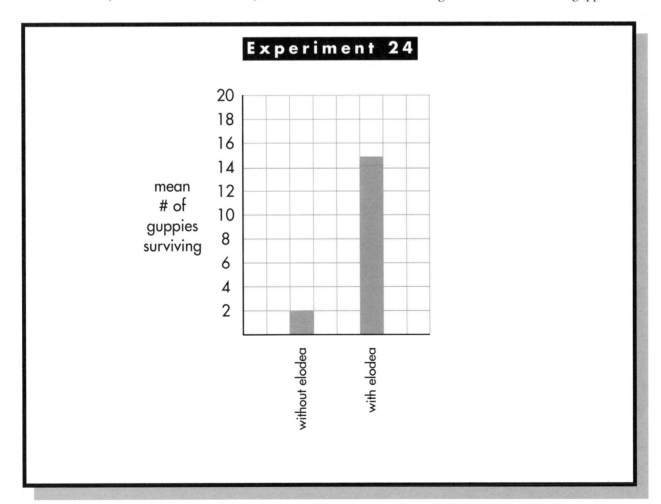

Experiment 24—One possible outcome, using three aquariums with elodea and three aquariums without elodea.

Check the guppies in the aquariums with no plants at frequent intervals, every 5 to 10 minutes. When the number of surviving guppies is as low as zero or one or two in at least one of the plantless aquariums, stop the experiment by removing all the goldfish from all six aquariums. Now count how many guppies remain in each of the aquariums.

If the goldfish are slow to eat the guppies, start over with fewer guppies in each aquarium.

If you have only one aquarium or have trouble finding newborn guppies or big goldfish, you can do the six trials consecutively (one at a time). In this case, do the three plantless trials first. In the first of the three, record how much time is required for the number of guppies to be reduced to one. Use that time interval for all subsequent trials, regardless of how many guppies are alive after that time.

Unlike most fish, guppies give birth to live young. When you purchase adults, a plump female is probably already full of babies.

Results

If the plants have helped the guppies hide from the goldfish, there should be more guppies alive in the aquariums with plants than in the plantless ones after the same amount of time.

Record your tallies of surviving guppies on the provided worksheet.

Conclusion

This is where the children accept or reject their hypotheses, answer their question, and attempt to explain their results. Research has shown that dense vegetation does reduce the amount of predation on fish and on amphibian larvae. The predators can't find them or get to them as easily.

Identifying the Experimental Concepts

The **experimental variable** in this experiment is the presence or absence of plants. We're asking whether the presence of plants affects the guppies' chance of survival.

The **control** in this case is the trials without plants. We're asking whether the presence of plants affects the guppies' survival.

The **dependent variable** is the number of guppies surviving in the aquariums. We're hypothesizing this is dependent upon the presence or absence of fish.

The **controlled variable**s are the factors that could vary between the plant trials and the no-plant trials, but are not allowed to vary. We have to use aquariums of the same size, the same type of plants, same type of guppies, same water temperature, same absence of outside disturbance, and so on.

The need for **multiple trials** is met by having three trials both with and without plants.

Extension

Can other items in the aquariums have the same effect? Can plastic plants? What about ceramic castles and other structures that are sold in pet stores to decorate fish aquariums?

Name: _____

Experiment 24

Question: Do goldfish eat fewer guppies when there is elodea throughout the aquarium?

Hypothesis: I think _____

_____

Materials: _____   _____

_____   _____

Procedure: We filled six aquariums with water. Then we filled three of those with elodea. We put twenty guppies into each aquarium. After an hour, we put two goldfish into each aquarium. We frequently counted the guppies in the three plantless aquariums until only one or two guppies were left. Then we removed all the goldfish from each of the six aquariums. We counted the remaining guppies in each aquarium.

Results: Number of guppies surviving in each aquarium

With Elodea	Without Elodea
_____	_____
_____	_____
_____	_____

Total
(or average): _____   _____

Conclusion: _____

_____

_____

Copyright © 1999 Sally Kneidel • Classroom Critters and the Scientific Method • Fulcrum Publishing • (800) 992-2908 • www.fulcrum-resources.com

Experiment 25

Question

Are Guppies More Attracted to Hiding Places When Predators Are Present?

Hypothesis

I think guppies are / are not more attracted to hiding places when predators are present.

Materials

- one aquarium
- a piece of chicken wire big enough to divide the aquarium across the center, with an additional inch along each side to fold over, to hold it in place
- 10 to 20 guppies or other fish smaller than goldfish, and small enough to swim through the chicken wire freely
- two goldfish, too large to fit through the chicken wire
- some sort of aquatic plant, such as elodea or hornwort, that will not float or sink but will remain suspended in the water column in the aquarium

Procedure

Put the chicken wire across the width of the aquarium, in the center, so that it divides the two ends of the aquarium into two equal halves. If you fold about an inch of each side edge at a right angle, the resulting one-inch flap will lie flat against the glass and will help hold the chicken wire in place. The chicken wire partition must be at least as high as the water is deep. Fill the aquarium with water. Add drops from the pet store to dechlorinate it. Purchase at a pet store, or remove from a pond, enough elodea or hornwort to more or less fill one half of the aquarium. There should still be room enough for the guppies to swim freely among or under the plants. The chicken wire will keep the plants on one side, but the guppies will be able to swim through the chicken wire.

To begin the experiment, introduce the guppies to the aquarium, five on the side with the plants, and five on the other side. After one hour, tally the number of guppies left on the plantless

Jessica records the position of the fish in the terrarium.

side. Are they more or less evenly distributed throughout the aquarium? Or are most of them clustered on one side? Repeat the tally every hour until you have at least three tallies (up to ten tallies), recording your tallies on the data sheet. After you've made three to ten tallies of the guppies' positions, introduce one or two goldfish to the plantless side of the aquarium. Try to get goldfish that are too big to go through the chicken wire. Otherwise, they may spend all their time on the plant side. An hour after you put the goldfish into the tank, tally the number of guppies left with the goldfish on the plantless side of the aquarium. If you have any suspicion that the goldfish may have eaten some guppies, remove the elodea and record how many are on the side with the plants, too. Return the plants and replace any guppies that were eaten. After another hour, repeat your tally. Keep on until you have at least three tallies with the goldfish, up to ten tallies. If your tallies are very consistent with each other, then three tallies may be enough. Does the presence of goldfish send the guppies into the side with plants?

Results

To the instructor or the children, depending on ages: Figure out the average number of guppies on the plantless side before the goldfish were added. If you did three trials and tallied two, five, and three guppies, then your average would be 3.3. Then calculate the average number of guppies on the plantless side after the goldfish were added. If some of the guppies were eaten in any particular trial, then calculate the proportion or percentage that were on the plantless side. For example, if only seven guppies survived a particular trial, and two were on the plantless side, then 2/7 (2 divided by 7) or .29 (29 percent) were on the plantless side. Using proportions or percentages will enable you to compare the before-goldfish tallies with the after-goldfish tallies, even though the total number of fish in the aquarium was not the same in the two types of trials.

You may want to figure out the average proportion for the before-goldfish trials and the average proportion for after-goldfish trials. For example, if you had the proportions of .27, .43, and .50 on the

plantless side before the goldfish was added, the average proportion would be 1.20/3 = .40. This would mean that 40 percent of the guppies were on the plantless side when no goldfish were in the aquarium.

Conclusion

This is where you accept or reject your hypothesis, answer your question, and attempt to explain your results. Why might small fish be more likely to move into vegetation when potential predators are present? Research has shown that dense vegetation does reduce the amount of predation on fish and on amphibian larvae. The predators can't find them or get to them as easily. Even though this strategy would probably help most aquatic prey to survive, that doesn't mean that all small fish stay hidden among plants. Some small fish may have evolved in habitats where there were no predators. If there were no predators, there would be no advantage to

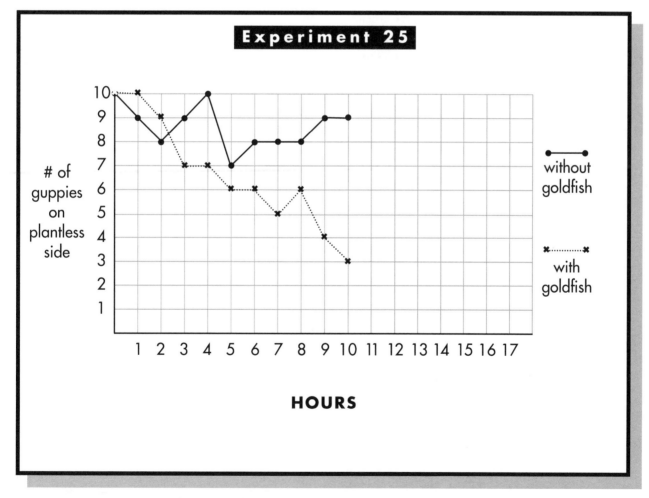

Experiment 25—A way to graph one possible outcome, starting with ten guppies for each trial (one trial with goldfish, one trial without goldfish).

hiding in weeds; hence, such a tendency would not be selected for. That is, those that didn't hide would survive and reproduce just as well as those that did. Or perhaps you found that the small fish hid in the weeds even when the goldfish were not present. It may be that the small fish don't actually recognize potential predators, but hide in the weeds all the time. This is the case for lots of prey, such as mice and earthworms, which never come out of their burrows except to forage for food. Would most fish species need to come out of the weeds to forage for food? No. Most of their food in nature, small insects and worms, etc., is probably more abundant in the weeds anyway. So why come out?

Identifying the Experimental Concepts

The **experimental variable** in this experiment is the presence or absence of the goldfish. We're asking whether the presence of a predator affects the guppies' choice of location.

The **control** in this case is the trials in the absence of goldfish. We're asking whether the presence of goldfish, a potential predator, causes the guppies to go into the vegetation, so we need to know what they do without predators.

The **dependent variable** is the number or proportion of guppies on the plantless side of the aquarium. We're hypothesizing that this is dependent upon the presence or absence of goldfish.

The **controlled variables** are the factors that could vary between the goldfish trials and the no-goldfish trials, but are not allowed to vary. We have to use the same aquarium, the same partition, the same plants, same type of guppies, same water temperature, same absence of outside disturbance, and so on.

The need for **multiple trials** is met by having three to ten trials both with and without goldfish.

Extension

Find out how goldfish behave when given a choice. Put elodea and/or hornwort on one side of the chicken wire as before. Add several goldfish that are small enough to pass through the chicken wire—only goldfish, no other fish. Tally their positions every hour for at least three hours.

Extension

As a variation of the extension above, put in one goldfish (either side) too big to pass through the chicken wire and one goldfish small enough to pass through, but too big for the other one to eat. Then tally every hour whether the small goldfish chooses to stay on the same side of the chicken wire as the big one. You don't need plants for this one.

Extension

If the small fish do spend more time among the plants when goldfish are present, do they show the same response to other threats? How do they respond to a fish model? To a hand in the water? To any foreign object in the water?

Name: _____

Experiment 25

Question: Are guppies more attracted to hiding places when predators are present?

Hypothesis: I think _____

_____

Materials: _____   _____

_____   _____

Methods: We put a partition of chicken wire across the middle of an aquarium. We then put elodea on one side of the partition only. We introduced ten guppies into the aquarium, on the plantless side. At one-hour intervals, we counted the number of guppies remaining on the plantless side for a total of _____ hours. Then we put two goldfish into the plantless side of the aquarium. We made an hourly count of the number of guppies on the plantless side, as before.

Results:

Number of guppies on plantless side **without** goldfish

Hour 1	_____	_____
Hour 2	_____	_____
Hour 3	_____	_____
Hour 4	_____	_____
Hour 5	_____	_____
Total	_____	_____

Number of guppies on plantless side **with** goldfish

Hour 1	_____	_____
Hour 2	_____	_____
Hour 3	_____	_____
Hour 4	_____	_____
Hour 5	_____	_____
Total	_____	_____

Conclusion: _____

_____

Copyright © 1999 Sally Kneidel • *Classroom Critters and the Scientific Method* • Fulcrum Publishing • (800) 992-2908 • www.fulcrum-resources.com

Experiment 26

Question
Do Fish Seek Out the Company of Other Fish?

Hypothesis
I think fish will / will not seek out the company of other fish.

Materials
- one or more aquarium fish
- one small aquarium or other container per pair of fish
- dechlorinated water
- paper or Plexiglas for making a grid
- one clock

Procedure
I buy feeder fish from a pet store. Specify that you want feeder fish, because they're much cheaper than pet fish, although they may look identical. Feeder fish are normally sold as food for larger fish or pet snakes.

You will need an aquarium at least 20 inches by 10 inches. Make a straight line at least 10 inches long on a piece of paper. Place the paper under the aquarium so that the line divides the aquarium into two equal halves. The line should be perpendicular to the length of the aquarium, so each half is roughly a square, not a long thin rectangle. If your aquarium has an opaque floor, you can make a line on a clear sheet of Plexiglas and put it over the aquarium. Or you can use a thin line of tape or a grease pencil to make a line on the side of the aquarium. Label the two halves of the aquarium A and B. Add dechlorinated water to the aquarium. Put in one fish, making sure the temperature of the water is the same as the water it came from. Use a premoistened fish net or premoistened hands to transfer the fish. Record the fish's position (either A or B) every 15 minutes for an hour. Repeat this on two subsequent days.

Then add a second fish, one that is roughly the same size but looks different enough to tell them apart. (Many goldfish have black or white markings.) Record the position of each fish (A or B) every 15 minutes for an hour. Repeat this on two subsequent days.

Chekeya notes that the two goldfish are staying together for this tally.

When you begin an hour of recording, you won't record the location at the beginning of the hour, but only after 15, 30, 45, and 60 minutes have passed.

Results
Your original three hours of data, with one fish, will probably show the fish to be occupying the A half and the B half of the aquarium equally, more or less. This will establish that neither side of the aquarium is more desirable than the other. With the next set of observations, you want to determine whether the two fish are together in one half of the aquarium more often than you would expect by chance. If they're moving around independently of one another, then you'd expect them to be in the same half of the aquarium in roughly one half of the observations—in about six of the twelve observations. Record in your results how often the fish were together in one half, and how often the fish were in opposite halves. For example, your results might say that you observed the fish together eight times and apart four times. Of

course, the more observations you have, the more reliable your data will be. If the fish move around a lot, you could record their positions every 10 minutes or even every 5 minutes. With this much data, you could also answer this question: Did the original fish move around more when he had company or when he was alone? That is, how many times did the fish switch halves when he was alone, and how many times when he had company? (If a series of observations were A, A, B, A, A, B, B, B, B, A, B, A, then he switched six times during that series.)

Conclusion

In their conclusion, the children will either accept or reject their hypotheses. Then they should try to explain their results. Were the fish in the same half of the aquarium consistently? Or were they in opposite halves consistently? Or did they seem to be indifferent? Hanging out together could mean they were a male and female possibly interested in courtship. Sometimes fish move around in groups or schools because it decreases the risk of predation for any particular individual. Fish in an aquarium might occupy the same area because they all expect to be fed in that area, or because they're all attracted to some other aspect of the environment. What are reasons they might avoid one another? Fish can be territorial and aggressive. Or they could regard one another as potential predators.

Identifying the Experimental Concepts

The **experimental variable** in this experiment is the presence of a second fish. We're asking if the presence of a second fish affects a fish's choice of location. So our experimental trials are those with two fish in the aquarium.

The **control** is observing the solitary fish before adding a second fish.

The **dependent variable** is the behavior of the original fish in the presence of the second fish. We're hypothesizing that the second fish is either repelling or attracting the original fish.

The **controlled variables** are all the factors that could affect the position of the fish, but aren't allowed to. These are hands in the water, taps on the glass, objects in the water, feeding the fish from the same spot every day, and so on.

The need for **multiple trials** is met by doing several observations on three different days.

Extension

Another way to go about this experiment is to make a grid to place underneath the aquarium as in Experiment 24. Number each square in the grid. Every 5 minutes, record the number of the square that is directly under each fish. Do this for at least an hour. Then figure out the number of lines between the two fish for every observation. If they were in adjacent squares, then it would be one line. Diagonal squares are two lines apart (or you can count them as one, as long as you're consistent). This procedure will give you a rough estimate of the fish's distance from each other.

Extension

Does your fish react differently to a fish of a different species than itself?

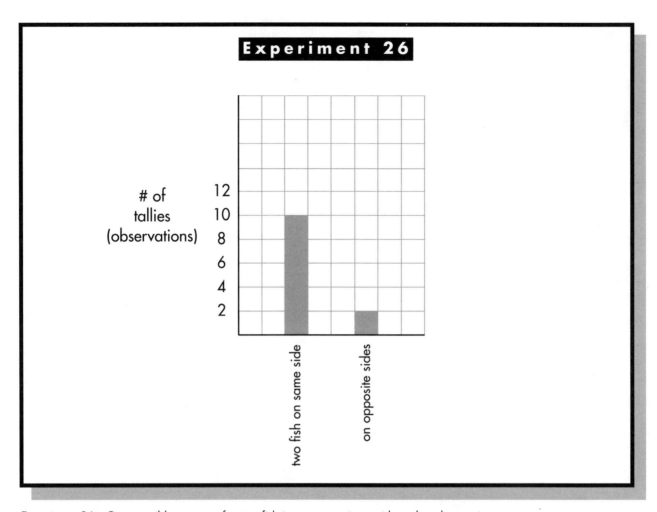

Experiment 26

of
tallies
(observations)

12
10
8
6
4
2

two fish on same side

on opposite sides

Experiment 26—One possible outcome for two fish in one aquarium, with twelve observations.

Name: _____

Experiment 26

Question: Do fish seek out the company of other fish?

Hypothesis: I think _____
_____

Materials: _____   _____
_____   _____

Procedure: We put a dark line on a piece of paper under the aquarium, dividing the aquarium visually in half. We labeled the two halves of the aquarium "A" and "B." We put one goldfish into the aquarium and recorded its position (either "A" or "B") every 15 minutes for an hour. We repeated this on two later days. We then added a second goldfish that looked different from the first, and recorded the position of each fish every 15 minutes for an hour, on three different days.

Results: Mark the position of the fish on the appropriate blanks.

		One goldfish in the aquarium		Two goldfish in the aquarium Goldfish 1		Goldfish 2		Are the fish on same side?	
		Side A	Side B	Side A	Side B	Side A	Side B	Yes	No
Day 1	15 min	___	___	___	___	___	___	___	___
	30 min	___	___	___	___	___	___	___	___
	45 min	___	___	___	___	___	___	___	___
	60 min	___	___	___	___	___	___	___	___
Day 2	15 min	___	___	___	___	___	___	___	___
	30 min	___	___	___	___	___	___	___	___
	45 min	___	___	___	___	___	___	___	___
	60 min	___	___	___	___	___	___	___	___
Day 3	15 min	___	___	___	___	___	___	___	___
	30 min	___	___	___	___	___	___	___	___
	45 min	___	___	___	___	___	___	___	___
	60 min	___	___	___	___	___	___	___	___
	Total	___	___	___	___	___	___	___	___

Conclusion: _____
_____

Copyright © 1999 Sally Kneidel • Classroom Critters and the Scientific Method • Fulcrum Publishing • (800) 992-2908 • www.fulcrum-resources.com

Experiment 27

Question

Can a Goldfish Be Trained to Come to Your Hand for Food?

Hypothesis

I think goldfish can /cannot be trained to come to my hand for food.

Materials

- at least one goldfish
- one aquarium at least 15 inches (37 cm) long
- fish food

Procedure

This experiment is more suitable for an individual or a whole group than for small groups, because it's longer than most. Consistency is important. One option is to have one individual (the teacher, perhaps) do the actual feeding while the children make hypotheses in advance and record data. Only one or two people can record data accurately at one time, since it requires looking down on the aquarium, although others can watch.

To do the control trials, you'll need to have a goldfish that hasn't already learned to come to a hand. You'll probably want at least ten observations for both the control trials and for the experimental trials. Designate one corner of the aquarium as your experimental area. Draw a square approximately 5 inches by 5 inches (13 cm x 13 cm) on a sheet of paper. Then place the drawn square underneath the experimental corner of the aquarium so that two sides of the square are directly underneath two sides of the aquarium.

The purpose of the control is to verify that the fish does not already have an attraction to the corner of the aquarium where the square is. To make the control observations, select in advance ten times when the children will observe and record the location of the fish, times when it is not being fed. Specifically, they'll be recording whether the fish is inside the drawn square in the experimental corner, when viewed from above, at the time of the observation. If you have enough time, do these at the same time on ten different days. If not, make them at least an hour apart or two hours apart to make sure that each observation is independent of the previous observation. During the time before and between the control observations, do what you can to avoid letting the fish see a person's hand or even a person's face at the time he receives his food. Turn the lights off when you feed him. Or cover his aquarium with an opaque cover, with a tiny hole for dropping the food through. Or dump his food into the aquarium with a little scoop on a long pole. Or you may be able to place the food on the end of a meter stick and turn the stick, dumping the food onto the water.

After you have at least ten control observations, it's time to begin training the fish. Now when you get ready to feed the fish, rest your hand on the side of aquarium and hold the food directly over the experimental square, above the water. But don't release the food. After 30 seconds, record the position of the fish. Is he in the square or out? Now wait until the fish is facing you, regardless of where he is in the aquarium, and release the food over the square. Repeat this procedure every time you feed the fish for the next couple of weeks: (1) first placing your hand over the square, (2) then recording the fish's position, (3) waiting until the fish can see you, and (4) then releasing the food over the square. Does anything change? Does he begin to enter the square after you've placed your hand there, but before you've released the food?

Results

The results are a statement of the number of times the fish was inside the square during the control trials and the number of times he was inside the square during the experimental trials. If he entered the square only after day 10 of the experimental trials, you might want to continue on for several more days and divide your experimental trials into two chunks of data—before and after the tenth day. This would show that there was a change over time after the training began.

Conclusion

Here the children accept or reject their hypotheses, and explain the results. Why did the fish begin to enter the square at the sight of your hand? This is an example of operant conditioning, a type of learning studied by an American psychologist named B. F. Skinner. In operant conditioning, an animal learns to associate its behavioral response with a reward or punishment. This kind of learning is important in both animals and humans. Although we regard fish as rather primitive creatures, they are vertebrates, just as we are. They have a capacity for learning that might exceed our expectations.

Identifying the Experimental Concepts

The **experimental variable** is the factor that's different between the control trials and the experimental trials, so in this case it would be feeding the goldfish with your hand over the square while the fish is watching. We're hypothesizing that this action eventually will cause the goldfish to swim to the square in response to the sight of your hand.

The **control** is observing the fish on ten different occasions to see how it responds to the square before you try to train it.

The **dependent variable** is the behavior of the fish in relation to the square, after you've begun feeding it over the square.

The **controlled variables** are those things that possibly could affect the behavior of the fish but are not allowed to. For example, the size, position, and color of the square remain the same, and the species of fish remains the same.

The need for **multiple trials** is met by making ten control observations and at least ten observations after the experimental training begins.

Extension

Design another experiment that involves this kind of training. How could you teach a mouse to come to a corner of his cage at the sight of a red glove? How could you teach a mouse to come to a corner of his cage at the sound of a buzzer?

Extension

Do the experiment according to the original design (ten control trials, ten experimental trials) with this variation: For the control, hold a small flashlight directly over the square for 10 seconds previous to recording the fish's location (that is, whether he is in or out of the square). Point the light beam into the water somewhat but away from the fish; it might hurt his eyes. He shouldn't have any reason to be attracted to the flashlight (you're not feeding him) and probably will not be. Now you'll see if you can train him to come to it, by shining the light before you feed him. Hold the same flashlight in the same manner over the square for 10 seconds. Then turn the flashlight off, record his position, and immediately drop the food into the water over the square. After doing this several times, does he begin to come toward the light before he sees your hand or the food?

Name: _____

Experiment 27

Question: Can a goldfish be trained to come to your hand for food?

Hypothesis: I think _____

_____

Materials:_____   _____

_____   _____

Procedure: We drew a 5 inch by 5 inch (13 cm x 13 cm) square on a piece of paper under one corner of an aquarium. We put our fish into the new aquarium. Then we selected ten test times, at least an hour apart, when we would record whether the fish was inside the square, when viewed from above. We recorded those ten observations (control observations). This was to show that the fish was not already attracted to that corner of the aquarium. Then we began feeding our fish from that same corner every day. We recorded the fish's position (whether it was in or out of the square) each day just *prior* to feeding, while a hand was over the square but the food held had not yet been released. Then we compared these observations to the control.

Results: Indicate the fish's position in the provided blanks:

	Control		While a hand is over the corner	
Obs.	Fish in square	Fish out of square	Fish in square	Fish out of square
1	_____	_____	_____	_____
2	_____	_____	_____	_____
3	_____	_____	_____	_____
4	_____	_____	_____	_____
5	_____	_____	_____	_____
6	_____	_____	_____	_____
7	_____	_____	_____	_____
8	_____	_____	_____	_____
9	_____	_____	_____	_____
10	_____	_____	_____	_____

Conclusion: _____

Copyright © 1999 Sally Kneidel • Classroom Critters and the Scientific Method • Fulcrum Publishing • (800) 992-2908 • www.fulcrum-resources.com

Experiment 28

Question

Can a Goldfish Be Trained to Touch a Black Circle in Response to a Hand Signal?

Hypothesis

I think I can / cannot train a goldfish to touch a black circle in response to a hand signal.

Materials

- at least one goldfish
- one aquarium

Procedure

Like Experiment 27, this experiment is more suitable for an individual or as a whole group activity than for several small groups, because it requires one aquarium per fish and because it's drawn out over a period of time. The procedures can be divided among groups or individuals; if so, make sure there is consistency. Another option is to have the children make predictions and record the data while the teacher does the actual feeding during the experimental trials.

To set up the aquarium, make a black paper circle about an inch in diameter and tape it to the outside of the aquarium a couple of inches from one corner, just below the water's surface.

You'll probably want at least ten observations for both the control trials and the experimental trials. To make the control observations, select in advance ten times when the children will observe and record the location of the fish. These times should be at least an hour or two apart. At the time of each control observation, note the position of the fish in relation to the black circle. Estimate the distance. If estimation is too difficult or not accurate enough, you can draw in advance a grid of one-inch (2.5 cm) squares. Put the paper with the grid under the aquarium so the children can see the grid from above. The control observations are for the purpose of demonstrating that the fish does not have any innate urge to touch the black circle (or maybe he does).

During the control observations, do what you can to avoid letting the fish see a person's hand or even a person's face at the time he receives his food. Turn the lights off when you feed him. Or cover his aquarium with an opaque cover, with a tiny hole for dropping the food through. Or dump his food into the aquarium with a little scoop on a long pole. Or you may be able to place the food on the end of a meter stick and turn the stick, dumping the food onto the water. If you don't do any of these things, at least avoid any consistency in the position of your hand at feeding time so that you won't be giving him training that is counter to the experimental trials.

After you have at least ten control observations, it's time to begin training the fish. You're going to begin rewarding the fish for closer and closer approaches to the black circle. On day one, rest your hand with the food on the edge of the aquarium over the black circle. After 30 seconds, record the fish's distance from the black circle. Then wait until the fish faces you and release the food.

On the second day, again rest your hand with the food over the black circle and, after 30 seconds, record the fish's distance from the black circle. After you've done that, wait to release the food until the fish is not only looking at your hand but is also making a move in your direction. On every subsequent day, begin once again by resting your hand on the side of the aquarium (over the black circle), waiting 30 seconds, then record the fish's distance from the circle. That part stays the same every day. What varies is when you release the food.

On day three, wait to release the food until the fish makes a more extensive move in your direction.

On day four, wait until the fish goes even closer toward your hand and the black circle before releasing the food. Eventually you'll be waiting until the fish is right at the black circle, even touching it, before releasing the food. When you get to this point, continue this procedure every day to reinforce the behavior. Now the children can show off the trained fish to a visitor, "Look, our fish will touch the black circle in response to a hand signal!" The hand signal is resting a hand over the circle (no food needed), in the same position as when you're getting ready to feed it. When the fish sees the hand, it should swim to the black circle. (Some fish seem to recognize individuals—the hand signal may need to be given by the person who feeds the fish.)

Results

The results are a statement of the control results (how close the fish got to the black circle during the control observations) and of the experimental results. Did the fish get closer and closer to the circle during the experimental trials?

Conclusion

The children either accept or reject their hypotheses. Did the fish respond to "rewarding" him with food for coming closer to the black circle? Why do many animals learn to change their behavior if it means getting food? Why is food rewarding for them?

Identifying the Experimental Concepts

The **experimental variable** is the factor that's different between the control trials and the experimental trials, so in this case it would be feeding the goldfish when he makes successively more pronounced movements toward the black circle while the feeder's hand is in view. We're hypothesizing that the action eventually will cause the goldfish to touch the black circle in response to the sight of the hand.

The **control** is observing the fish on ten different occasions to see how it responds to the black circle before you begin to train it.

The **dependent variable** is the behavior of the fish in relation to the black circle after you've begun to feed it over the circle.

The **controlled variables** are those things that possibly could affect the behavior of the fish but are not allowed to. For example, the size, position, and color of the circle remain the same, and the species of fish remains the same.

The need for **multiple trials** is met by making ten control observations and at least ten observations after the experimental training begins.

Extension

Do you think you could teach a fish to come to a black circle that was on the opposite side of the aquarium from where he was fed? Do you think it would take longer than the experiment above? Describe how you would go about it. Could you teach a mouse to press a lever to get food? Describe how you would do it if you had access to any materials you needed.

Extension

Vary the hand signal. See if you can train the fish to come to a finger snap.

Name: _____

Experiment 28

Question: Can a goldfish be trained to touch a black circle in response to a hand signal?

Hypothesis: I think _____
_____

Materials: _____ _____
_____ _____

Procedure: We taped a black circle to the outside of an aquarium, 2 inches from a corner and below the water's surface. We put a 1-inch grid under the aquarium. Then on ten prescheduled occasions, we recorded the fish's distance from the circle. Next we began to train the fish. One person rested a hand, with fish food, on the edge of the tank over the black circle. After 30 seconds, we recorded the fish's position. Then, when the fish was looking, the food was dropped. We repeated the procedure daily, but waiting on each successive day until the fish was a little closer to the black circle before releasing the food. Finally, the fish had to be touching the black circle before the food was released. After several days of repetitions, we showed that the fish would touch the circle in response to a hand over the circle, even when there was no food.

Results: Distance between fish and circle

Observation	Before being trained	While being trained
1	_____	_____
2	_____	_____
3	_____	_____
4	_____	_____
5	_____	_____
6	_____	_____
7	_____	_____
8	_____	_____
9	_____	_____
10	_____	_____

Conclusion: _____
_____
_____

Copyright © 1999 Sally Kneidel • Classroom Critters and the Scientific Method • Fulcrum Publishing • (800) 992-2908 • www.fulcrum-resources.com

CHAPTER 3

Anolis Lizards (Anoles)

Question

Do Anoles Prefer Mealworms or Crickets?

Hypothesis

I think anoles prefer mealworms / crickets.

Materials

- at least one Carolina anole (commonly available at pet stores)
- at least one terrarium
- mealworms
- crickets

Procedure

Carolina anoles are smart enough to have individual behaviors and individual preferences in some respects. You can't always generalize completely from one lizard to all others of the same species. Some Carolina anoles won't eat in captivity at all. You can do this experiment by asking about anoles in general. Or, if you have only one anole to test, then change the question to: Does our or my Carolina anole prefer mealworms or crickets?

There are a couple of ways to measure an animal's preference for a food item. One is to count the number of such items eaten over an extended period of time, assuming that the animal has access to many more than it eats. Another way is to measure, on several occasions, the amount of time that elapses between the time an item is offered and the time it is eaten. Still another way is to repeatedly offer two different food items in pairs, and record which is eaten first each time.

Anoles often don't eat food items right way. Probably the easiest way to conduct this experiment with an anole is to offer food items in pairs (one cricket and one mealworm). Then check every hour or so until one of the items is eaten. If both items are eaten after an hour, check sooner next time. One cricket or one mealworm a day is plenty to sustain an anole. If

Emily and Alan wait for the lizard to make his choice.

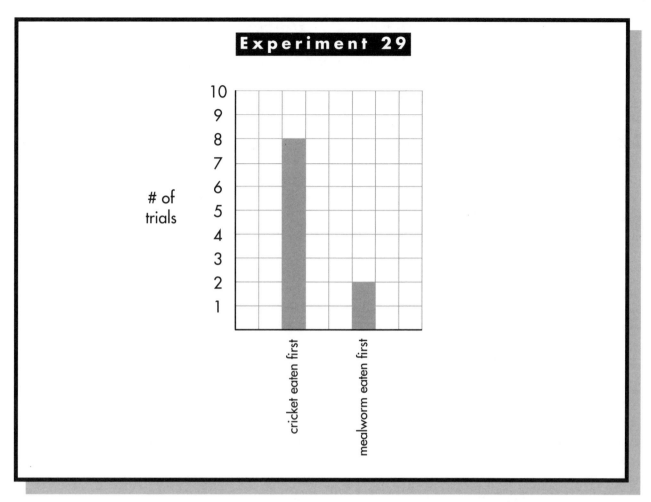

Experiment 29

# of trials

cricket eaten first

mealworm eaten first

Experiment 29—One possible outcome of ten trials with one lizard.

the lizard has been well fed all along, it probably won't eat more than that. So do only one trial per day for a week or ten days. Also keep in mind that an average-sized anole probably won't eat an adult cricket, or a full-sized mealworm. Many pet stores sell cricket nymphs, or immature crickets. About 3/8 inch (1 cm) is the optimum size for crickets as adult anole prey. To keep the sizes balanced, choose mealworms that are about the same size, up to 5/8 inch in length. Ideally, you want to house each anole separately so you'll know who's doing the eating. Another consideration is that when several anoles are housed together, some individuals may be too intimidated to eat at all.

If you do have several anoles housed together, you can simply put in, say, ten crickets and ten mealworms at the same time. Check back every hour and record how many of each have been eaten, until all of one prey type is gone.

The terrarium floor should be kept bare during this experiment so all prey items remain equally visible. Spray the inner terrarium walls with a plant mister a couple of times a day, creating a few heavy drops on the glass. The lizard will lap at the drops for water. If the cricket remains uneaten long enough for dehydration to be a problem, leave a moist, somewhat crumpled paper towel in the terrarium overnight.

Results

The children's results are a statement of how many crickets were eaten versus how many mealworms were eaten. They would also include any observations about how the lizards noticed, pursued, caught, and swallowed prey.

Conclusion

In the conclusion, the children accept or reject their hypotheses, then try to explain their results.

Was one species of prey more wiggly than another species? Did the lizards obviously notice one prey type more quickly than another? Was one type easier to catch than another? Was one easier to swallow than another?

Identifying the Experimental Concepts

The **experimental variable** here is the variation in the identity of the prey items.

The **control** in this experiment is having two types of prey. We can't say anything about anoles' relative preference for crickets without also offering them another type of prey that they are known to eat.

In this experiment as written above, the **dependent variable** is the number of each prey type consumed, which depends upon which one anoles like better, or notice more readily, or can catch more easily.

The **controlled variables** are the factors that could affect prey choice but aren't allowed to. We control for prey size by choosing mealworms and crickets of approximately the same size. We introduce the prey in the same way and at the same distance from the lizard, making sure both are in plain sight.

The need for **multiple trials** is met by offering seven to ten prey items of each type.

Extension

Do anoles take fewer crickets when mealworms are also present? In this case, we'd offer the anoles crickets alone in the first trials, recording how quickly the crickets were eaten or how many crickets were eaten over a given period of time. Then we'd offer crickets and mealworms simultaneously and record again how long it took for the crickets to be eaten or how many crickets were eaten. Then we'd compare the counts for the two situations. In such an experiment, the control would be the number of crickets eaten, or the time elapsed before eating them, in the absence of mealworms. We'd be asking how the presence of mealworms affected the consumption of crickets. In such an experiment, the dependent variable would be the number of crickets consumed, which would depend upon the presence or absence of mealworms.

Extension

What other prey items will the lizard accept? Try ants, small grasshoppers, small flies, small pill bugs, small earthworms, small spiders, and any other small animals you can find other than bees or wasps. If you have an insect net, sweep it through tall grass (not grass that has been chemically treated) and dump the entire contents in with your lizard. Keep track of which items he eats first.

Name: _____

Experiment 29

Question: Do anoles prefer mealworms or crickets?

Hypothesis: I think _____

_____

Materials: _____   _____

_____   _____

Procedure: We offered our anole one small cricket and one small mealworm about the same size. We recorded which was eaten first. We repeated this procedure nine more times.

Results: Which was eaten first?

	Cricket	Mealworm
Trial 1	_____	_____
2	_____	_____
3	_____	_____
4	_____	_____
5	_____	_____
6	_____	_____
7	_____	_____
8	_____	_____
9	_____	_____
10	_____	_____

Conclusion: _____

_____

_____

_____

Copyright © 1999 Sally Kneidel • Classroom Critters and the Scientific Method • Fulcrum Publishing • (800) 992-2908 • www.fulcrum-resources.com

Experiment 30

Question

How Do Male Anoles Respond to Their Own Image in a Mirror?

Hypothesis

I think male anoles will not react / will react by …

Materials

- one male anole
- one terrarium
- one mirror at least 4 inches by 4 inches (10 cm x 10 cm)
- a similarly sized but nonreflective square of some other material, perhaps cardboard

Procedure

One child easily can do this experiment alone. If you're in a classroom and have only one lizard, children can make individual hypotheses, then

Alan admires the lizard after putting the mirror in place.

observe as a whole group. There's more observation involved here than there is actual manipulation of materials. If you have enough lizards and terraria and mirrors, then small groups of children can each set up their own experimental terraria and observe in small groups.

To prepare for the control trials, tape the nonreflective square to the outside of the terrarium glass, at a level where the lizard can see it. It must be perfectly vertical, not at an angle. The children should observe the lizard for the next hour or two afterwards. They can watch him while doing other things. At least one person should stop to give him full attention if he approaches the nonreflective square. Have someone write down anything he does that seems to be directed to or related to the square.

Repeat the above setup and observation instructions for the experimental trial, except replace the nonreflective square with a mirror. The mirror, particularly, must be perfectly vertical, not at a slant, or the lizard will not be able to see his reflection. If there is a favorite resting place for the lizard in the terrarium, such as at the top of a branched stick, you can put the mirror where he'll see it clearly from that spot. You can use a small amount of clear packing tape to attach it to the side of the terrarium. (Opaque packing tape can block out light around the mirror.) If you have a mirror with a flat bottom that will stand by itself without tape, that will work.

Don't leave the mirror in place for long periods, unless the lizard has not yet noticed it. The presence of the image is probably stressful to him.

Results

Adult male Carolina anoles will respond to their own image in a mirror. They respond with a color change (green to brown or black) and a change in general body shape (a side-to-side flattening that causes a ridge of skin to rise along the neck and back, making the anole look bigger from the side). A long, fan-shaped flap of skin will descend from the throat, which also makes the anole look bigger from the side and is a flashy bright pink. Behavioral changes will include doing push-ups with the front legs, making the shoulders and head bob up and down.

This is one experiment where the results probably will not be in numbers or measurements, unless the children notice a particular behavioral display that they can count, such as the number of push-ups per minute.

Conclusion

In the conclusion, the children either accept or reject their hypotheses. Then they explain their results. Why does the male react this way to his reflection in a mirror? He reacts as if his reflection is another male. Male anoles are territorial; they defend an area of turf as their own. They have signals to let other males know that they have blundered into claimed territory. The color change is a signal that the resident male is in his own territory and is feeling defensive of his territory. The change in body shape makes the resident look bigger and more menacing to intruders. This may not happen until the provocation has gone on for some time. The head bobbing is a direct behavioral communication that means "Get out of here."

Identifying the Experimental Concepts

The **experimental variable** here is the presence or absence of a mirror. We're asking about the effect of the mirror on the lizard's behavior.

The **control** is also observing the lizard's behavior when there is no mirror present; rather, there is a square foreign object present that's the same shape and size as the mirror.

The **dependent variable** is the behavior of the lizard, which we're hypothesizing depends upon the presence of the mirror.

The **controlled variables** are those things that could be different between the observations with the

A kitten stares at the lizard, which is out of view of the camera, at the top of the stick. Note the mirror attached to the side of the aquarium.

cardboard and those with the mirror—things that could affect the lizard's behavior. We keep them the same so they won't affect the lizard's behavior—Such things as the contents of the terrarium, the absence of other lizards in the terrarium, and distractions outside the terrarium.

The need for **multiple trials** is not addressed in this experimental design. You would need to repeat both the control and the experimental trial with the mirror at least twice, for a total of three each, to have good replication. I didn't suggest that here because the lizard's reaction to the mirror, when he does react, is so dramatic that it will be obvious he's reacting to the mirror. You can replicate the trials for form's sake, but you won't need to in order to be convinced that your results are real.

Extension

Will a female Carolina anole respond to her image in a mirror? Will a lizard of another species? What about another species of anole, such as the knight anole? Will a male Carolina anole react to another male Carolina anole in exactly the same way that he reacted to the mirror?

Name: _____

Experiment 30

Question: How do male anoles respond to their own image in a mirror?

Hypothesis: I think _____

_____

Materials: _____   _____

_____   _____

Procedure: We taped a nonreflective square to the outside of our terrarium and observed the anole's reaction to it. Then we taped a mirror to the outside of the terrarium, where he could see it. We watched and recorded the lizard's reaction to the mirror.

Results: Reaction to nonreflective square: _____

_____

_____

_____

_____

Reaction to mirror: _____

_____

_____

_____

_____

Conclusion: _____

_____

_____

_____

Copyright © 1999 Sally Kneidel • Classroom Critters and the Scientific Method • Fulcrum Publishing • (800) 992-2908 • www.fulcrum-resources.com

Experiment 31

Question

Will a Male Anole Respond to a Photograph of Another Male, or Does the Image Have to Be Moving?

Hypothesis

I think male anoles will / will not respond to a photograph of another male anole of the same species.

Materials

- one male Carolina anole
- one terrarium
- a good quality, life-size color photograph of a male Carolina anole with his pink throat fan extended (make a color photocopy from a reptile field guide or other book)
- one mirror at least 4 inches by 4 inches (10cm x 10cm) or a second male Carolina anole

Procedure

For the control, tape the mirror to the outside of the terrarium glass, at a level where the lizard can see it. It must be perfectly vertical, not at an angle. Have the children observe the lizard for the next hour or two. They can take turns watching him, or they can watch him while doing other things, giving him their full attention if he approaches the mirror. They should write down anything he does that seems to be directed to or related to the mirror. The purpose of this control is to make sure that your lizard will react to a moving image. If he doesn't react to that, then he surely won't react to a photograph.

Repeat the above procedure for the experimental trial, except replace the mirror with a sharp, color, life-size photograph of a male anole of the same species. The photograph, like the mirror, should be perfectly vertical. If there is a favorite resting place for the lizard in the terrarium, such as at the top of a branched stick, you can put the mirror, then the photograph, where he'll see it clearly from that spot. You can use a small amount of clear packing tape to attach each in turn to the side of the terrarium. If the photograph seems clearer on the inside of the glass, then put it on the inside.

Repeat the observations with both the mirror and the photograph if the outcome is uncertain.

Don't leave the mirror in place for long periods. The presence of the image is stressful to a male. If he reacts to the photograph, don't leave that in place for long either.

Results

Adult male Carolina anoles will respond to their own image in a mirror. They respond with a color change (green to brown or black) and a change in general body shape (a side-to-side flattening that causes a ridge to form along the neck and back). A long, fan-shaped flap of skin, called a dewlap, descends from the throat, which makes the anole look bigger from the side and is a flashy pink. Behavioral changes include doing push-ups with the front legs, making the shoulders and head bob up and down.

If the anole reacts to the photograph, is his reaction exactly the same as to the mirror?

This is one experiment where the results probably will not be in numbers or measurements, unless the children want to count a particular behavioral display, such as the number of push-ups per minute.

Conclusion

In the conclusion, the children either accept or reject their own hypotheses. Then they explain their results. What is the difference between the image in the mirror and in the photograph? A male anole reacts to a mirror as if his reflection is another male. Male anoles are territorial; each defends an area of turf as his own. He sees the image in the mirror as a male in his territory who needs to be driven out. But when he bobs at the image in the mirror to signal "Get lost," the image bobs back at him! This challenge heightens his efforts to expel the intruder. But the more vehement the anole gets in his territorial displays, the more vehement his perceived challenger gets, too! This is why the mirror is stressful to a male—his signals are not effective in chasing away the challenger. They seem only to provoke the intruder to greater heights of rudeness. The anole in the photograph does have the extended dewlap, an aggressive signal, but at least it doesn't bob back at him. So even if he does respond to the photograph, he may not respond as aggressively.

Identifying the Experimental Concepts

The **experimental variable** here is the presence of the photograph versus the mirror. We're asking about the effect of the photograph on the lizard's behavior, as compared to the effect of the mirror.

The **control** is observing the lizard's reaction to the mirror.

The **dependent variable** is the behavior of the lizard, which we're hypothesizing depends upon the presence of the photograph as opposed to the mirror.

The **controlled variables** are those things that could be different between the observations with the mirror and those with the photograph—things that could affect the lizard's reaction. We keep them the same so they won't affect his reaction. These are such things as the contents of the terrarium, the absence of other lizards in the terrarium, distractions outside the terrarium, and the size of the image.

The need for **multiple trials** is not addressed in the experimental design above. You would need to repeat both the control and the experimental trial with the photograph at least twice, for a total of three each, to have good replication.

Extension

Does a male react to a photograph of a calm male, with no dewlap extended? Does he react to a drawing of a male with a dewlap exaggerated in color or size or both?

Experiment 31

Question: Will a male anole respond to a photograph of another male, or does the image have to be moving?

Hypothesis: I think _____

_____

Materials:_____   _____

_____   _____

Procedure: We taped a mirror to the terrarium wall in a place where our male anole would be likely to see it. We observed him for _____ minutes and recorded any reactions to the mirror. Then we replaced the mirror with a photograph of an anole of the same species. Again we observed him for _____ minutes and recorded any reactions to the photo.

Results: Reaction to mirror: _____

_____

_____

_____

_____

Reaction to photo: _____

_____

_____

_____

_____

Conclusion: _____

_____

_____

_____

Copyright © 1999 Sally Kneidel • Classroom Critters and the Scientific Method • Fulcrum Publishing • (800) 992-2908 • www.fulcrum-resources.com

Experiment 32

Question

Will an Anole Change Color in Response to a Color Change in Its Surroundings?

Hypothesis

I think an anole will / will not change color in response to a change in the color of its surroundings.

Materials

- at least one male or female Carolina anole
- one terrarium
- branches with brown leaves, small enough to fit into the terrarium
- branches with green leaves, small enough to fit into the terrarium
- green paper
- brown paper

Procedure

This experiment involves several sets of observations. So, if you have a class and only one lizard, you might want to divide up the observation periods among groups of children. Then everyone gets a job but no one has to watch for hours.

Before you test the anole's reaction to an environmental color change, you need to get some baseline or control information. You need to determine how frequently anoles change color in the absence of any environmental color change or disturbance. To do this, have the children observe and record the anole's color every 5 minutes for an hour, on two or three different days. How many times did its color change per hour, on the average? Did it change at all?

Next you need to determine whether human activity in the terrarium, such as the act of moving branches around, is enough to prompt a color change, regardless of the color of the branches. First have the children observe and record the color of the anole every five minutes for 30 minutes. Then place a branch with green leaves in the terrarium, one that has enough leaves to more or less surround the lizard with the green color. Again, have the children observe and record the color of the anole every five minutes for 30 minutes. Now remove the branches with green leaves

and replace them with other branches that also have green leaves. Again, have the children observe and record the color of the anole every 5 minutes for 30 minutes. Ideally, you should repeat this test of the effect of disturbance twice more. If time is a problem, omit the repetitions.

The two above procedures were both control trials. Now you're ready for the experimental trials. Again have the children observe and record the color of the anole every 5 minutes for 30 minutes. Then install some branches with leaves that are the opposite colors of the anole's skin. If his skin is green, put in a branch with brown leaves. If his skin is brown, put in a branch with green leaves. The branches should have enough leaves to more or less surround the anole with green or brown, without touching him. After you've done that, have the children observe and record the color of his skin every 5 minutes for 30 minutes. Now switch the color of the leaves. If you had a branch with brown leaves, put in one with green leaves. If you had a branch with green leaves, put

Alan puts green leaves into the terrarium.

in one with brown leaves. Again, observe and record the anole's color every 5 minutes for 30 minutes.

Unless the outcome is very clear, repeat the procedure in the above paragraph two more times.

Results

The results are a statement of which situation produced the most color changes. If you observed the same number of color changes in all three situations, then the data suggest that neither environmental color change nor disturbance provokes a color change in the anoles. If the two types of trials that involved moving branches produced a color change, whereas the first trial did not, then the data suggest that disturbance, rather than a change in environmental color, provokes a color change. If the experimental trial, where the color of the leaves was changed, was the only trial where a color change in the lizards occurred, then the data suggest that a change in the environment can induce a change in color of the lizards.

Conclusion

Here the children accept or reject their hypotheses. Then they attempt to explain what they observed. For a long time, people have believed that anoles change color in response to their environment, to blend in more fully with their background. It's true that anoles are usually green or brown, and they are usually in a green or brown environment. Those are the most common colors of nature, and most animals are colored for camouflage. But recently, it has been suggested that anoles' color change is actually a reflection of either their emotional state or their body temperature. You learned in Experiments 30 and 31 that an anole will turn brown in response to a territorial challenge. Brown signals aggression to other lizards. But why would a lizard change color in response to environmental temperature? Lighter colors reflect more light. This helps an animal stay cool. Dark colors absorb light, which tends to warm a dark animal or object. A black road in summer will be much hotter than a white sidewalk. So if a lizard's body is too cool, changing to a darker

brown skin color will help him absorb light and heat. If his body is warmer than is comfortable, changing to a light green will reflect light and thus help him cool off.

Identifying the Experimental Concepts

The **experimental variable** here is changing the color of the leaves in the terrarium. We're hypothesizing that will change the color of the lizard's skin color.

The **control** is (1) observing any color changes in the lizard that occur when you're not changing anything in the terrarium, and (2) observing any color changes that occur as a result of simply changing branches in the terrarium (a disturbance). These two procedures control for the possibility that anoles change colors frequently at random for no reason, or that they change colors in response to any sort of environmental change or disturbance. Having carried out these control trials and observed no color changes, we then can say that a lizard color change after a change in the color of the leaves must be due to the change in color of the leaves.

The **dependent variable** is the change or lack of change in the lizard following the change in color of the leaves.

The **controlled variables** are any factors that could change during the course of the experiment and that might affect the color of the lizard, such as disturbance by students, changes in other bright colors around the terrarium, changes in temperature during the experiment, and the presence of other anoles in the terrarium or within sight of the terrarium. All of these factors are controlled—we keep them from changing during the course of the experiment so they won't affect the outcome.

The need for **multiple trials** is met, if needed, by repeating the two types of control trials, and the experimental trials twice, for a total of three runs each.

Extension

Repeat the experiment using colored paper instead of brown and green leaves. You might try taping sheets of construction paper all over the inside of the terrarium, except the top.

Extension

Design an experiment to test the effect of environmental temperature on the color of anoles. Do not exceed extremes of 90 degrees and 50 degrees Fahrenheit.

Name: _____

Experiment 32

Question: Will an anole change color in response to a color change in its surroundings?

Hypothesis: I think _____

_____

Materials:_____ _____

_____ _____

Procedure: We did three kinds of trials: (1) control trials with no disturbance or environmental color change, (2) trials with a disturbance but no environmental change, and (3) trials with both a disturbance and an environmental color change. For the control, we observed and recorded our anole's color every 5 minutes for an hour on _____ different days. Next we tested the effect of disturbance alone on the anole's color. We observed the anole's color every 5 minutes for 30 minutes. We then replaced those branches with some other green ones and observed again, every 5 minutes for 30 minutes. Finally, for the experimental trials, we began by observing the anole's color every 5 minutes for a total of 30 minutes. Then we added to the terrarium some branches with _____ (green or brown) leaves—the opposite of our anole's color at that time. We observed and recorded the color of the anole every 5 minutes for a total of 30 minutes. Then we removed the branches and put in branches of the opposite color, again observing the color of the anole every 5 minutes for a total of 30 minutes.

Results: Control trials

# min.	Trial 1 Anole color	Trial 2 Anole color	Trial 3 Anole color
5	_____	_____	_____
10	_____	_____	_____
15	_____	_____	_____
20	_____	_____	_____

Experiment 32 (continued)

Copyright © 1999 Sally Kneidel • *Classroom Critters and the Scientific Method* • Fulcrum Publishing • (800) 992-2908 • www.fulcrum-resources.com

Experiment 32 (continued)

# min.	Trial 1 Anole color	Trial 2 Anole color	Trial 3 Anole color
25	_____	_____	_____
30	_____	_____	_____
35	_____	_____	_____
40	_____	_____	_____
45	_____	_____	_____
50	_____	_____	_____
55	_____	_____	_____
60	_____	_____	_____

Testing the effect of disturbance with no environmental color change:

# min.	Anole color	After adding green leaves: # min.	Anole color	After replacing with more green leaves: # min.	Anole color
5	_____	5	_____	5	_____
10	_____	10	_____	10	_____
15	_____	15	_____	15	_____
20	_____	20	_____	20	_____
25	_____	25	_____	25	_____
30	_____	30	_____	30	_____

Testing the effect of environmental color change:

# min.	Anole color	After adding _____ leaves: # min.	Anole color	After replacing with _____ leaves: # min.	Anole color
5	_____	5	_____	5	_____
10	_____	10	_____	10	_____
15	_____	15	_____	15	_____
20	_____	20	_____	20	_____
25	_____	25	_____	25	_____
30	_____	30	_____	30	_____

Experiment 32 (continued)

Copyright © 1999 Sally Kneidel • *Classroom Critters and the Scientific Method* • Fulcrum Publishing • (800) 992-2908 • www.fulcrum-resources.com

Experiment 32 (continued)

# min.	Anole color	After adding _____leaves:		After replacing with _____leaves:	
		# min.	Anole color	# min.	Anole color
5	_____	5	_____	5	_____
10	_____	10	_____	10	_____
15	_____	15	_____	15	_____
20	_____	20	_____	20	_____
25	_____	25	_____	25	_____
30	_____	30	_____	30	_____

# min.	Anole color	After adding _____leaves:		After replacing with _____leaves:	
		# min.	Anole color	# min.	Anole color
5	_____	5	_____	5	_____
10	_____	10	_____	10	_____
15	_____	15	_____	15	_____
20	_____	20	_____	20	_____
25	_____	25	_____	25	_____
30	_____	30	_____	30	_____

Conclusion: _____

_____

_____

_____

_____

_____

_____

Copyright © 1999 Sally Kneidel • Classroom Critters and the Scientific Method • Fulcrum Publishing • (800) 992-2908 • www.fulcrum-resources.com

CHAPTER 4

Kittens and Puppies

Question

Do Kittens Prefer Human Contact More Than Cats Do?

Hypothesis

I think kittens prefer human contact more than /
less than / the same amount as cats do.

Materials

- one to three kittens
- one to three cats
- one empty and clean plastic wading pool (dry),
  or a comparable confined area

Procedure

Since this experiment requires a confined area,
such as a wading pool, you'll probably conduct
only one trial at a time. With a class, you could do
the entire experiment as a whole group activity,
or you could divide the children into groups and
have each group do one trial. The setting for this
experiment should be a confined area big enough
to accommodate a child and a cat, and big
enough to give the cat a choice between empty
space and a human lap. But it should not be so
big that the kitten or cat wanders away, exploring, and forgets about the child. A good setting
might be a plastic wading pool, of any size.

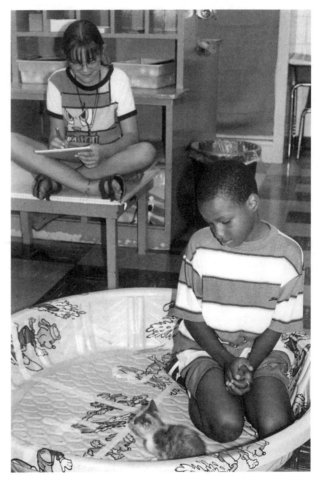

Becca makes another tally as Brandon looks longingly at
the kitten. This pool is divided into numbered quadrants.
The numbers are masking tape.

Before having the child and the first animal
enter the pool, divide the pool floor into four
equal-sized quadrants by drawing on the pool
floor or by laying down masking tape. (Some

Sara records tallies, Alan calls out the time, and Becca sits motionless watching the kitten. This pool is divided into halves rather than quadrants.

pools have a clear plastic film over the whole pool that can tear when you remove the tape.) When everyone is ready to begin, have the child sit within one of the four quadrants, with his or her back against the edge of the pool. Instruct the child to sit still, not to touch the animal or beckon to it in any way, and to keep quiet. Begin with a kitten, which will probably be easier. Place the kitten in the quadrant opposite the child, far from the child. Have the children who are collecting data watch the kitten for 20 minutes, recording every 60 seconds which quadrant the kitten is in. When the kitten is in the same quadrant as the child, have them also record whether the kitten is making physical contact with the child, and what kind of contact.

If your pool is small or your child is large, you can divide the pool into halves rather than quadrants. The worksheet can be used either way.

Repeat this procedure two more times, using a different kitten and person each time, if possible.

Now start over with a cat in place of the kitten. You may need to surround the pool with something to contain the cat. A series of standing science project boards can provide high walls around the pool. If the cat can't be contained in the pool, you might try using a small room for the experiment instead of the pool. Divide the floor of the room into quadrants. Or you can do the experiment with only the kitten, asking instead, "Does a kitten prefer human company or solitude?"

Results

The results will be, for both the kitten and the cat, the total number of tallies for each quadrant. If an animal is indifferent to the human, then we expect it to be in the same quadrant as the human in one-quarter of the observations. If it is avoiding the human, it will be in the same quadrant less than one-quarter of the time. If it is seeking the company of the human, then we expect to see it in the same quadrant as the human more than one-quarter of the time. Which did you observe for the kitten? For the cat? Were they different? If you recorded tallies every minute for three 20-minute periods, you'll have 60 tallies for the kitten and 60 tallies for the cat. Roughly 15 tallies in the human quadrant, out of 60, indicates indifference on the part of the animal.

Conclusion

Here the children accept or reject their hypotheses, and try to explain their results. Did the three 20-minute trials for the kitten produce similar tallies? If not, if the three trials were very different from each other, you probably need to do more trials, until you begin to see consistency. Why might kittens behave differently than cats? Do you think other young domestic animals might behave the same way?

Identifying the Experimental Concepts

The **experimental variable** here is the age of the feline. We're asking about the difference in the behavior of a kitten and a cat.

If we're asking about the reaction of the kitten, then the **control** is testing the cat. We need the reaction of the cat as a comparison.

The **dependent variable** is the amount of time spent with the child—the proportion of tallies in which the kitten and child were together. We're hypothesizing that this depends upon the age of the kitten or cat (whether it's an adult or not).

The **controlled variables** are those factors that might affect the outcome but are not allowed to. For example, people outside the pool shouldn't distract the animal or call to it in any of the trials. If you use a room for the cat instead of a pool, you should use a room for the kitten as well if you intend to compare the two sets of trials.

The need for **multiple trials** is met by doing at least three 20-minute trials with a kitten, and three with a cat, and even more if necessary for consistency of outcome.

Sara cuddles up with a new friend.

Extension

Does familiarity with the human make a difference? If you have a friend who owns a kitten, do three trials with the owner of the kitten sitting in as the human in the pool, and three more trials with a person the kitten doesn't know. Was the proportion of tallies in the human quadrant different for the two sets of trials?

Extension

Do you think trials with a nondomestic animal or a cold-blooded animal might produce different results? Try the experiment with a hermit crab or a pet snake or lizard.

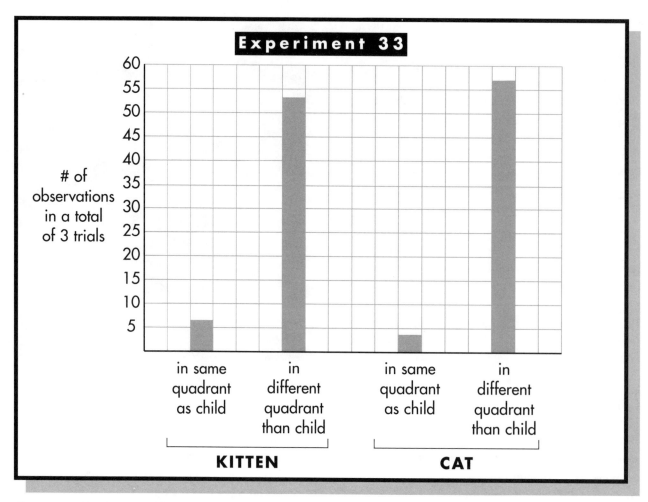

Experiment 33—One possible outcome, with three trials of twenty observations each. Each observation includes both a kitten and a cat.

Name: _____

Experiment 33

Question: Do kittens prefer human contact more than cats do?

Hypothesis: I think _____

_____

Materials: _____   _____

_____   _____

Procedure: We divided a wading pool into four quadrants. One person sat in one quadrant. We placed a kitten in a different quadrant. We recorded whether the kitten was in the same quadrant as the person, or in a different quadrant, once a minute for a total of 20 minutes. We repeated this for two more 20-minute periods. Then we replaced the kitten with a cat and did three 20-minute observation periods in exactly the same way with the cat instead.

Results:

KITTEN							CAT					
Trial 1		**Trial 2**		**Trial 3**			**Trial 1**		**Trial 2**		**Trial 3**	
Same quad.	Diff. quad.	Same quad.	Diff. quad.	Same quad.	Diff. quad.		Same quad.	Diff. quad.	Same quad.	Diff. quad.	Same quad.	Diff. quad.
___	___	___	___	___	___		___	___	___	___	___	___
___	___	___	___	___	___		___	___	___	___	___	___
___	___	___	___	___	___		___	___	___	___	___	___
___	___	___	___	___	___		___	___	___	___	___	___
___	___	___	___	___	___		___	___	___	___	___	___
___	___	___	___	___	___		___	___	___	___	___	___
___	___	___	___	___	___		___	___	___	___	___	___
___	___	___	___	___	___		___	___	___	___	___	___
___	___	___	___	___	___		___	___	___	___	___	___
___	___	___	___	___	___		___	___	___	___	___	___

Experiment 33 (continued)

Copyright © 1999 Sally Kneidel • *Classroom Critters and the Scientific Method* • Fulcrum Publishing • (800) 992-2908 • www.fulcrum-resources.com

Experiment 33 (continued)

KITTEN						CAT					
Trial 1		**Trial 2**		**Trial 3**		**Trial 1**		**Trial 2**		**Trial 3**	
Same quad.	Diff. quad.	Same quad.	Diff. quad.	Same quad.	Diff. quad.	Same quad.	Diff. quad.	Same quad.	Diff. quad.	Same quad.	Diff. quad.
___	___	___	___	___	___	___	___	___	___	___	___
___	___	___	___	___	___	___	___	___	___	___	___
___	___	___	___	___	___	___	___	___	___	___	___
___	___	___	___	___	___	___	___	___	___	___	___
___	___	___	___	___	___	___	___	___	___	___	___
___	___	___	___	___	___	___	___	___	___	___	___
___	___	___	___	___	___	___	___	___	___	___	___
___	___	___	___	___	___	___	___	___	___	___	___
___	___	___	___	___	___	___	___	___	___	___	___
___	___	___	___	___	___	___	___	___	___	___	___

Totals

KITTEN

# of observations of kitten and person in same
quadrant, summed over the three trials   _____

# of observations of kitten and person in different
quadrants, summed over the three trials   _____

CAT

# of observations of cat and person in same
quadrant, summed over the three trials   _____

# of observations of cat and person in different
quadrants, summed over the three trials   _____

Conclusion: _____

_____

_____

_____

Copyright © 1999 Sally Kneidel • Classroom Critters Snd the Scientific Method • Fulcrum Publishing • (800) 992-2908 • www.fulcrum-resources.com

Experiment 34

Question

Which Chooses Human Contact More—a Kitten or a Puppy?

Hypothesis

I think puppies prefer human contact more than / less than / the same amount as kittens do.

Materials

- one to three puppies of a small breed
- one to three kittens
- one empty and clean plastic wading pool (dry), or a comparable confined area

Procedure

The setting for this experiment should be a confined area big enough to accommodate a person and a puppy or kitten, and big enough to give the animal a choice between empty space and a human lap. But it should not be so big that the animal wanders away, exploring, and forgets about the human. A good setting might be a plastic wading pool, a small fenced-in enclosure, or a small room.

Before having the child and the first animal enter the enclosure, divide the floor of the enclosure into four equal-sized quadrants by drawing lines or by laying down masking tape or string (removing masking tape later may pull the plastic coating off a small pool.)

When you are ready to begin, have the child sit within one of the four quadrants, with his or her back against the edge. Instruct the child to sit still, not to touch the animal or beckon to it in any way, and to keep quiet. Begin with the kitten, unless you already have data on the kitten from the preceding experiment. Place the kitten in the quadrant opposite the child, far from the child. Have the children who are collecting data watch the kitten for 20 minutes, recording every 60 seconds which quadrant the kitten is in. When the kitten is in the same quadrant as the child in the enclosure, also record whether the kitten is making physical contact with the child, and what kind of contact.

Sara watches without encouraging the puppy, who seems to prefer human contact. This pool is divided into halves.

Repeat this procedure two more times, using a different kitten and child each time, if possible.

Now start over with a puppy in place of the kitten. Do three trials with the puppy, as you did with the kitten.

If your pool is small, you can divide it into halves rather than quadrants. It doesn't really matter. You can use the worksheet either way.

Results

The results will be, for both the kitten and the puppy, the total number of tallies for each quadrant. If an animal is indifferent to the child, then we expect it to be in the same quadrant as the child in one-quarter of the observations. If it is avoiding the child, it would be in the same quadrant less than one-quarter of the time. If it is seeking the company of the child, then we expect to see it in the same quadrant as the child more than one-quarter of the time. (If you divided the space into halves instead of quadrants, then change the fractions in the three preceding sentences to one-half. Which did the children observe for the kitten? For the puppy? Were the observations different? If tallies were recorded every minute for three 20-minute periods, then the data sheet will have sixty tallies for the kitten and sixty tallies for the puppy. Roughly 15 tallies in the human quadrant, out of 60, would indicate indifference on the part of the animal. Or if you divide the space into halves, then 30 tallies with human contact, out of 60, indicates indifference.

Conclusion

Here the children accept or reject their hypotheses, and try to explain their results. Did each of the three 20-minute trials for the kitten produce similar tallies? If not, if the three trials for the kitten were very different from one another, then you probably need to do more trials, until you begin to see consistency. Likewise for the puppy.

Were the puppy and the kitten different? Why might we expect them to be different?

Identifying the Experimental Concepts

The **experimental variable** here is the species of the baby animal. We're asking about the difference in the behavior of a kitten and a puppy.

If we focus on the reaction of the puppy, then the **control** is also testing the kitten. We need the reaction of the kitten for comparison.

The **dependent variable** is the proportion of tallies for the quadrant containing the child. We're hypothesizing that this depends upon the species of animal being tested.

The **controlled variables** are those factors that might affect the outcome but are not allowed to. For example, people outside the pool shouldn't distract the animal or call to it in any of the trials. If you use a room for the puppy instead of a pool, then you should use a room for the kitten as well if you intend to compare the two sets of trials.

The need for **multiple trials** is met by doing at least three 20-minute trials with a kitten, and three with a puppy, more if necessary for consistency of outcome.

Extension

Repeat the experiment using a cat and a dog rather than a kitten and a puppy. Choose a dog similar in size to a cat so the relative size of the enclosure won't be markedly different. Also, familiarity can make a huge difference in a dog's response to a person, so either have all the animals in the study paired with their owners, or none. If you choose a person and dog that are unfamiliar with each other, be careful not to choose a dog that might be aggressive toward a stranger.

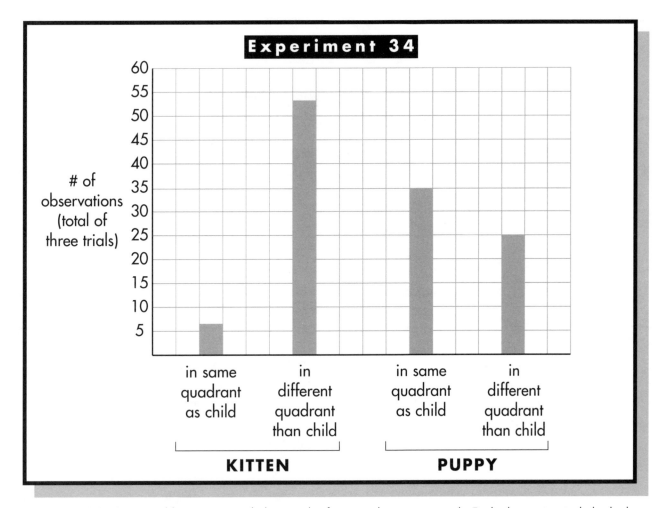

Experiment 34—One possible outcome, with three trials of twenty observations each. Each observation includes both a kitten and a puppy.

Name: _____

Experiment 34

Question: Which chooses human contact more—a kitten or a puppy?

Hypothesis: I think _____

_____

Materials: _____ _____

_____ _____

Procedure: We divided a wading pool into four quadrants. One person sat in one quadrant. We placed a kitten in a different quadrant. Then, for 20 minutes, we recorded every 60 seconds whether the kitten was in the same quadrant as the person or in a different quadrant. We repeated this procedure and the observations for two more 20-minute periods. Then we replaced the kitten with a puppy and did three 20-minute observations, in exactly the same way as we did with the kitten.

Results:

KITTEN						PUPPY					
Trial 1		**Trial 2**		**Trial 3**		**Trial 1**		**Trial 2**		**Trial 3**	
Same quad.	Diff. quad.	Same quad.	Diff. quad.	Same quad.	Diff. quad.	Same quad.	Diff. quad.	Same quad.	Diff. quad.	Same quad.	Diff. quad.
___	___	___	___	___	___	___	___	___	___	___	___
___	___	___	___	___	___	___	___	___	___	___	___
___	___	___	___	___	___	___	___	___	___	___	___
___	___	___	___	___	___	___	___	___	___	___	___
___	___	___	___	___	___	___	___	___	___	___	___
___	___	___	___	___	___	___	___	___	___	___	___
___	___	___	___	___	___	___	___	___	___	___	___
___	___	___	___	___	___	___	___	___	___	___	___

Experiment 34 (continued)

Copyright © 1999 Sally Kneidel • Classroom Critters and the Scientific Method • Fulcrum Publishing • (800) 992-2908 • www.fulcrum-resources.com

Experiment 34 (continued)

KITTEN						PUPPY					
Trial 1		**Trial 2**		**Trial 3**		**Trial 1**		**Trial 2**		**Trial 3**	
Same quad.	Diff. quad.	Same quad.	Diff. quad.	Same quad.	Diff. quad.	Same quad.	Diff. quad.	Same quad.	Diff. quad.	Same quad.	Diff. quad.
___	___	___	___	___	___	___	___	___	___	___	___
___	___	___	___	___	___	___	___	___	___	___	___
___	___	___	___	___	___	___	___	___	___	___	___
___	___	___	___	___	___	___	___	___	___	___	___
___	___	___	___	___	___	___	___	___	___	___	___
___	___	___	___	___	___	___	___	___	___	___	___
___	___	___	___	___	___	___	___	___	___	___	___
___	___	___	___	___	___	___	___	___	___	___	___
___	___	___	___	___	___	___	___	___	___	___	___
___	___	___	___	___	___	___	___	___	___	___	___
___	___	___	___	___	___	___	___	___	___	___	___

Totals

KITTEN

# of observations of kitten and person in same
quadrant, summed over the three trials   _____

# of observations of kitten and person in different
quadrants, summed over the three trials   _____

PUPPY

# of observations of puppy and person in same
quadrant, summed over the three trials   _____

# of observations of puppy and person in different
quadrants, summed over the three trials   _____

Conclusion: _____

_____

Copyright © 1999 Sally Kneidel • Classroom Critters and the Scientific Method • Fulcrum Publishing • (800) 992-2908 • www.fulcrum-resources.com

E x p e r i m e n t   3 5

Question

Is a Heated Stuffed Animal More Attractive to a Kitten for Company Than a Cool Stuffed Animal?

Hypothesis

I think the heated stuffed animal will be more attractive than / less attractive than / equally as attractive as the cool stuffed animal.

Materials

- a plush hand puppet, one that looks like a stuffed animal
- a hot-water bottle
- at least one kitten
- an enclosure such as a plastic wading pool (dry)

Procedure

First test the kitten's response to the puppet when the puppet is cool (room temperature). To begin, divide the floor of the enclosure into two equal-sized halves by drawing lines or laying down masking tape or string. Put a small towel or rag inside the puppet to fill it out, so it will sit up. Put it in the rear center of one half of the enclosure, as far as possible from the other half. When you are ready to begin, put the kitten in the half not containing the puppet. Have the children record every minute for 20 minutes which half the kitten is in. If it's in the half with the puppet, they should also record what the kitten does anytime it touches the puppet. Repeat this procedure twice more on two different days, or with two different kittens, for a total of three sessions.

For the next step, remove the towel from the puppet. Replace the towel with a hot water bottle containing hot water, hot enough and in a great enough quantity to warm the puppet. Prop up the puppet in one half, as before. Put the kitten in the opposite half. Once again have the children record which half of the pool the kitten is in every minute for 20 minutes. Repeat twice more for a total of three sessions.

You can divide the pool into quadrants instead of halves if you prefer. The worksheet is usable either way.

The kitten seems more interested in Becca's activities than in the puppet. This pool is divided into quadrants. Each quadrant has a masking tape number.

If the puppet is too small to accommodate a standard hot-water bottle, use instead an ice bag filled with hot water. Ice bags are more flexible. Test the ice bag first to make sure hot water won't rupture it. If you don't have either a hot-water bottle or an ice bag, use a jar.

Results

Did the kitten show more interest in the warm puppet than in the cool puppet? Or did it ignore both of them? If it was in the half of the pool with the puppet in more than half the observations, for either set of trials, then it may have been attracted to the stuffed animal. The results also include any observations of the kitten's reaction to the puppet, or lack of a reaction, in addition to the tallies.

Conclusion

In the conclusion, the children either accept or reject their hypotheses, then attempt to explain their results. Why might a kitten be attracted to a stuffed animal? Why might a kitten ignore one? Why might a warm stuffed animal be more attractive?

Identifying the Experimental Concepts

The **experimental variable** here is the warmth of the puppet. Does the heat affect the kitten's response to the puppet?

The **control** is the response of the kitten to the puppet when the puppet isn't warm. We're comparing the number of tallies near the puppet when the puppet was cool to the number of tallies near the puppet when the puppet was warm.

The **dependent variable** is the number of tallies of the kitten near the warm puppet. We're hypothesizing that this number depends upon the heat.

The **controlled variables** are those factors that could affect the outcome but aren't allowed to. For example, we have to use the same puppet in all trials, and it has to be sitting up in the same position all the time. We have to use the same pool and the same kitten, or if we use several kittens, they should be balanced in age between the control (cool puppet) and the experimental (warm puppet).

The need for **multiple trials** is met by doing three 20-minute trials with both the cool puppet and the warm puppet.

Extension

Would you expect a kitten to be more or less attracted to a warm stuffed animal than an adult cat might be? Why?

The kitten may be drawn to the stuffed animal more out of curiosity than out of a need for comfort. You might suspect this if the kitten sniffs the puppet but doesn't curl up next to it. What could you do to figure out what is motivating the kitten? What if you offered a rubber or plastic object about the same size as the puppet, but not at all soft or cuddly? You could tally the kitten's reaction to that and compare it to the kitten's reaction to the puppet.

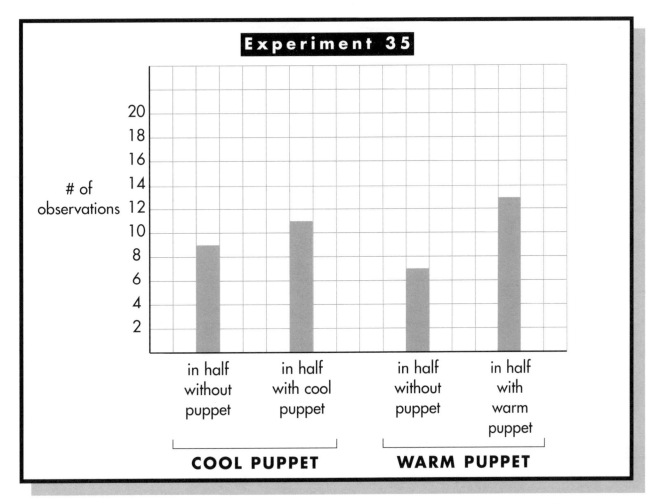

Experiment 35—One possible outcome, for one 20-minute trial with a room-temperature (cool) puppet and one 20-minute trial with a warm puppet.

Experiment 35

Question: Is a heated stuffed animal more attractive to a kitten for company than a cool stuffed animal?

Hypothesis: I think _____

_____

Materials: _____   _____

_____   _____

Procedure: We divided the enclosure into two halves. In one half we put a plush hand-puppet, stuffed with a towel or rag. We placed the kitten in the other half of the enclosure. We recorded every minute for 20 minutes which half the kitten was in. We repeated this procedure twice more. Then we stuffed the kitten with a hot water bottle, making it warm. Once again we recorded every minute for 20 minutes which half of the enclosure the kitten was in. We repeated this procedure twice more.

Results:

COOL PUPPET							WARM PUPPET					
Trial 1		**Trial 2**		**Trial 3**			**Trial 1**		**Trial 2**		**Trial 3**	
with puppet	without puppet	with puppet	without puppet	with puppet	without puppet		with puppet	without puppet	with puppet	without puppet	with puppet	without puppet
____	____	____	____	____	____		____	____	____	____	____	____
____	____	____	____	____	____		____	____	____	____	____	____
____	____	____	____	____	____		____	____	____	____	____	____
____	____	____	____	____	____		____	____	____	____	____	____
____	____	____	____	____	____		____	____	____	____	____	____
____	____	____	____	____	____		____	____	____	____	____	____
____	____	____	____	____	____		____	____	____	____	____	____
____	____	____	____	____	____		____	____	____	____	____	____
____	____	____	____	____	____		____	____	____	____	____	____

Experiment 35 (continued)

Copyright © 1999 Sally Kneidel • *Classroom Critters Sand the Scientific Method* • Fulcrum Publishing • (800) 992-2908 • www.fulcrum-resources.com

Experiment 35 (continued)

COOL PUPPET						WARM PUPPET					
Trial 1		**Trial 2**		**Trial 3**		**Trial 1**		**Trial 2**		**Trial 3**	
with puppet	without puppet	with puppet	without puppet	with puppet	without puppet	with puppet	without puppet	with puppet	without puppet	with puppet	without puppet
——	——	——	——	——	——	——	——	——	——	——	——
——	——	——	——	——	——	——	——	——	——	——	——
——	——	——	——	——	——	——	——	——	——	——	——
——	——	——	——	——	——	——	——	——	——	——	——
——	——	——	——	——	——	——	——	——	——	——	——
——	——	——	——	——	——	——	——	——	——	——	——
——	——	——	——	——	——	——	——	——	——	——	——
——	——	——	——	——	——	——	——	——	——	——	——
——	——	——	——	——	——	——	——	——	——	——	——
——	——	——	——	——	——	——	——	——	——	——	——
——	——	——	——	——	——	——	——	——	——	——	——
——	——	——	——	——	——	——	——	——	——	——	——

Totals

Conclusion: _____

_____

_____

_____

_____

_____

_____

_____

Copyright © 1999 Sally Kneidel • Classroom Critters and the Scientific Method • Fulcrum Publishing • (800) 992-2908 • www.fulcrum-resources.com

Experiment 36

Question

Will a Kitten Choose Another Kitten for Company?

Hypothesis

I think a kitten will / will not choose another kitten for company.

Materials

- two or more kittens that are not identical, designated as Kitten A, Kitten B, and so on, or by name
- one empty and clean plastic wading pool, or a comparable confined area

Procedure

A good setting might be a plastic wading pool (dry), a small fenced-in enclosure, or a small room. First divide the floor of the enclosure into two equal-sized halves by drawing a line or laying down masking tape or string. Number the halves "1" and "2" with tape or a marker. When you are ready to begin, put Kittens A and B in the pool, in opposite halves. Have the children watch the kittens for 20 minutes, recording every minute on the data sheet which half of the pool each kitten is in. When the kittens are in the same half, the children should also note whether the kittens are making physical contact with one another, and what kind of contact.

Have the children repeat this procedure two more times, using Kitten A once again, but with a new second kitten if possible.

You can divide the pool into quadrants instead of halves if you prefer. The worksheet is usable either way.

Results

The results will be the total number of tallies (observations) where Kitten A was in the same half of the pool as Kitten B, and the total number of tallies when the kittens were in opposite halves. If one or both of the kittens are attracted to the other, then we expect them to be in the same half of the pool more than 50 percent of the time. If one or both of the kittens are avoiding the other, then we expect them to be in the same half less than 50% of the time. If the kittens are indifferent to each other, then we expect them to be in the same half of the pool in about 50 percent of the observations. What was the case for your kittens? If tallies were recorded after every minute for three 20-minute periods, you'll have 60 tallies for the kittens on each completed data sheet. Roughly 30 tallies of the kittens in the same half of the pool, out of 60, would indicate indifference on the part of both kittens.

Conclusion

Here the children accept or reject their hypotheses, and try to explain their results. Did each of the three 20-minute trials for the kittens produce similar tallies? If not, if the three trials for the kittens were very different from each other, then you probably need to do more trials, until you begin to see consistency.

Why might kittens seek out one another?

Identifying the Experimental Concepts

The **experimental variable** in this experiment is the presence of a second kitten. We're asking how the presence of the second kitten affects the location of Kitten A.

The **control** here is contained within the experimental setting. We're asking whether Kitten A chooses the company of another kitten. Giving Kitten A the option of solitude, in the opposite half of the pool, is the control.

The **dependent variable** is the location of Kitten A relative to the second kitten. We're hypothesizing that Kitten A's location depends upon the presence and location of the second kitten.

The **controlled variables** are all the factors that could influence Kitten A's choice of location but which are being kept equal between the two halves of the enclosure. Those factors are the absence of food, a bed, water, toys, or any other object or animal.

The need for **multiple trials** is met by having at least three 20-minute trials.

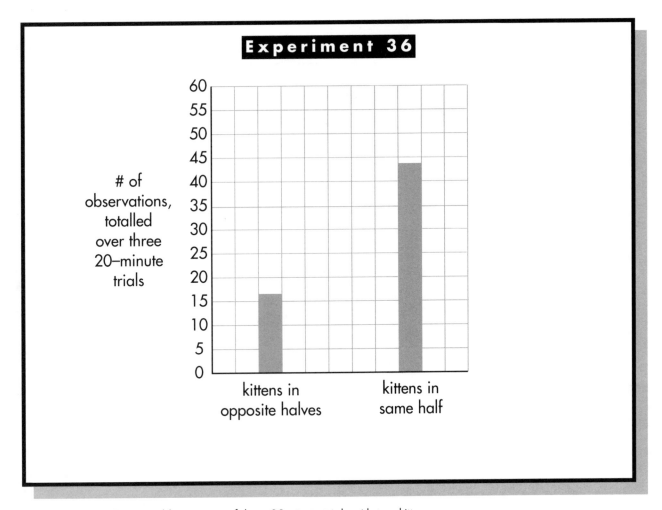

Experiment 36

# of observations, totalled over three 20–minute trials

kittens in opposite halves

kittens in same half

Experiment 36—One possible outcome of three 20-minute trials with two kittens.

Extension

Test Kitten A as above, with a wading pool (dry) or other enclosure divided into halves, but with no second kitten present. Record which half Kitten A is in, as before, every minute for 20 minutes, three times (three trials of 20 minutes' duration each).

Then add Kitten B and repeat. But this time restrain Kitten B with a collar and a leash attached to the side of the pool so Kitten B can't leave its side of the enclosure. Now record Kitten A's position every minute for 20 minutes, on three occasions. This is really a more rigorous test of the original hypothesis. Are the results the same?

Experiment 36

Question: Will a kitten choose another kitten for company?

Hypothesis: I think _____

_____

Materials: _____ _____

_____ _____

Procedure: We divided a dry plastic wading pool into two equal halves with tape and numbered the halves "1" and "2". We put Kittens A and B into the pool. We recorded which half each kitten was in every minute for three 20-minute observation periods. We noted also every minute whether the kittens were touching.

Results:

	Trial 1		Trial 2		Trial 3	
	Kitten A	Kitten B	Kitten A	Kitten B	Kitten A	Kitten B
1 min.	_____	_____	_____	_____	_____	_____
2 min.	_____	_____	_____	_____	_____	_____
3 min.	_____	_____	_____	_____	_____	_____
4 min.	_____	_____	_____	_____	_____	_____
5 min.	_____	_____	_____	_____	_____	_____
6 min.	_____	_____	_____	_____	_____	_____
7 min.	_____	_____	_____	_____	_____	_____
8 min.	_____	_____	_____	_____	_____	_____
9 min.	_____	_____	_____	_____	_____	_____
10 min.	_____	_____	_____	_____	_____	_____
11 min.	_____	_____	_____	_____	_____	_____
12 min.	_____	_____	_____	_____	_____	_____
13 min.	_____	_____	_____	_____	_____	_____
14 min.	_____	_____	_____	_____	_____	_____
15 min.	_____	_____	_____	_____	_____	_____
16 min.	_____	_____	_____	_____	_____	_____
17 min.	_____	_____	_____	_____	_____	_____
18 min.	_____	_____	_____	_____	_____	_____
19 min.	_____	_____	_____	_____	_____	_____
20 min.	_____	_____	_____	_____	_____	_____
Total	_____	_____	_____	_____	_____	_____

In how many of the observations were the kittens in the same half?   Different halves?

Conclusion: _____

_____

Copyright © 1999 Sally Kneidel • Classroom Critters and the Scientific Method • Fulcrum Publishing • (800) 992-2908 • www.fulcrum-resources.com

Experiment 37

Question
Do Kittens Show Left- or Right- Handedness?

Hypothesis
I think kittens will show left-handedness / right-handedness / neither.

Materials
- one to five kittens
- a small bit of a good-smelling canned cat food on a small square of foil, or other treat that a kitten wants badly (about nickel-sized, or maybe quarter-sized)
- a place to put the food so that the kitten can almost reach it with one paw but cannot get to it with his body (such as the space under a dresser)

Procedure
You can make an experimental space by supporting a rectangular or square board with two stacks of books, so the board is about 2 inches above the floor. You may have to make adjustments for the size of the kittens. With a seven-week-old kitten, a height of 1.75 inches worked for me. The board should be high enough, and the meat back far enough, that the kitten can almost reach the meat with one paw but not quite. The kitten should not be able to get its head under the shelf.

Let the kitten see and smell the piece of meat, then put the meat in place. Have the children tally which paw she uses for each effort. When the paw comes completely out from under the board, that completes one try; so that's one tally. If the kitten immediately tries again, that's another effort and a separate tally, as long as his paw was completely withdrawn from the overhang. You may need to let the kitten reach and eat the piece of meat every so often to keep his interest. Remember, if he gets full, he won't be interested. So keep the pieces of meat very small.

Ideally, you'll need at least three kittens. The more tallies you have, the better. Test each kitten in at least three different sessions, at least an hour apart. Continue each session as long as that kitten

The kitten goes for the treat with its left paw while Sara tallies. Emily considers pushing the treat a little farther back. The treat here is a bit of wet cat food on a piece of foil. This kitten used both paws equally in the first trial, but in later trials used the left paw predominantly.

is making efforts you can tally.

A preponderance of tallies for either the left paw or the right paw may indicate handedness in cats, or at least in the test cat.

If you have five or more kittens, the children may be able to draw some tentative conclusions about whether most cats have the same handedness, as in humans, where there's a predominance of right-handedness.

Results
The results are a statement of the total number of tries with the left paw and the total per right paw, for each session. In the results, the children would also record any relevant observations, such as whether and how often they had to let the kitten have the meat to keep his interest.

Conclusion
In the conclusion, the children accept or reject their hypotheses, and attempt to explain their results. Why might kittens use one front paw

more than another? Since cats and humans are both highly developed mammals, they have a lot of brain similarities. Humans show handedness because one brain hemisphere dominates the other. Perhaps it's the same in cats. Or if they don't show dominance with one paw, why might that be? Perhaps their paws are not dexterous or skilled enough to show a difference. A dominance in human feet is not as evident as the dominance in hands because our feet don't have as many fine motor skills that are noticeable.

Identifying the Experimental Concepts

There is no **experimental variable** here. It's not really an experiment but an observation, because we're not altering anything or causing anything to vary. To make this an experiment, you'd have to, for example, compare kittens and puppies. Then your experimental

variable would be the identity of the animal species. Or you could compare kittens to cats. Then your experimental variable would be the age of the animal.

There is no **control** here. To have a control, you'd have to have an experimental variable. For example, you could try to train a cat to use its right paw more by rewarding it for using that one (such as letting it keep the meat when retrieved with the right paw). Then you might compare the frequency of right-paw use in a trained cat to that of an untrained cat. In this example your sessions with the untrained cat would be the control. You would compare them to the sessions following training to tell you the effect of training.

There is no **dependent variable** here, because there is no experimental variable. In a sense, however, the relative number of tallies with the right paw and with the left paw is the dependent variable. It depends upon the preference, or lack of preference, of the cat.

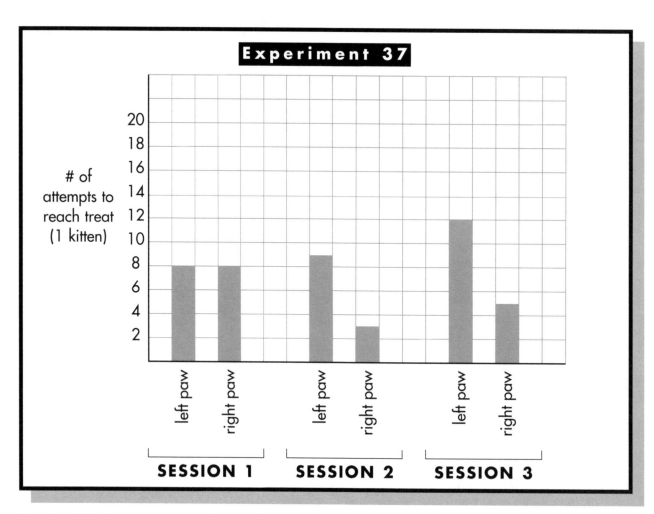

Experiment 37—Two ways to summarize possible outcomes in graphs.

The **controlled variables** are any variables, any factors, that could affect the outcome. For example, the age of the cats should be the same between sessions unless age is your experimental variable. As always, outside disturbances by observers should be consistently minimized in all sessions to avoid affecting the results.

The need for **multiple trials** is met by doing at least three trials with each kitten, with several tallies for each observation.

Extension

Several extensions are suggested in the discussion of experimental variable and control above. Another variation is to try the same experiment, just suspending a small piece of twisted paper on a string in front of a kitten, or dragging it along the floor in front of the kitten, and recording how many times the kitten bats at it with each paw.

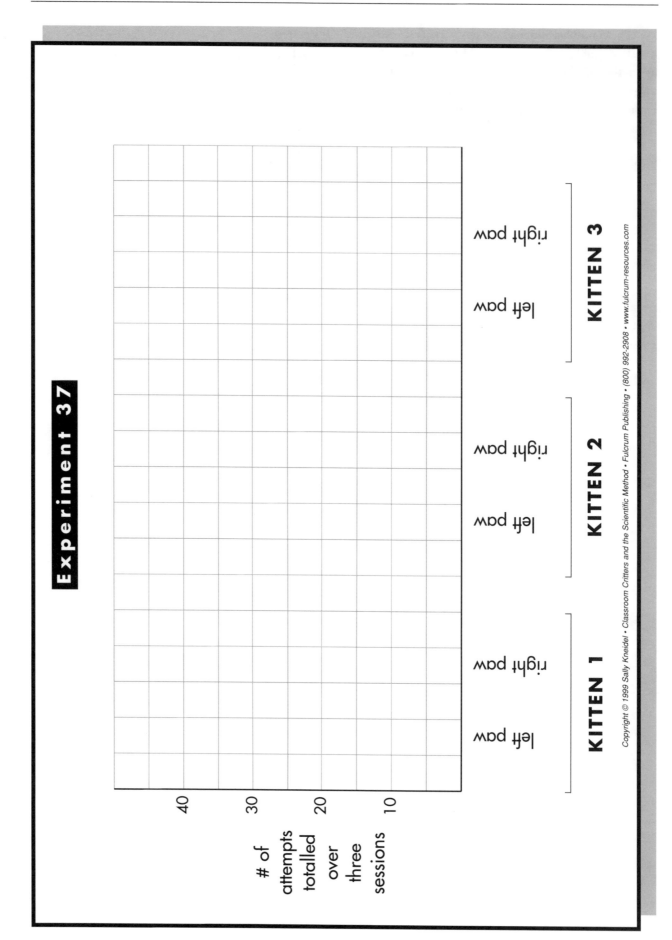

Experiment 37

# of attempts totalled over three sessions

40
30
20
10

KITTEN 1
left paw · right paw

KITTEN 2
left paw · right paw

KITTEN 3
left paw · right paw

Copyright © 1999 Sally Kneidel · Classroom Critters and the Scientific Method · Fulcrum Publishing · (800) 992-2908 · www.fulcrum-resources.com

Name: _____

Experiment 37

Question: Do kittens show left- or right-handedness?

Hypothesis: I think _____

_____

Materials: _____   _____

_____   _____

Procedure: We made a little shelf around 2 inches off the floor. We tested each of three kittens separately, three sessions for each kitten. To begin each session, we placed a small piece of meat under the shelf, just out of reach of the kitten being tested. Then we put the kitten in front of the shelf, showed her the meat and tallied how many times she used each paw to reach for it. We continued the session until the kitten lost interest.

Results: Tally the number of tries with each paw.

	Kitten 1		**Kitten 2**		**Kitten 3**	
	left paw	right paw	left paw	right paw	left paw	right paw
Session 1	_____	_____	_____	_____	_____	_____
Session 2	_____	_____	_____	_____	_____	_____
Session 3	_____	_____	_____	_____	_____	_____
Total	_____	_____	_____	_____	_____	_____

Conclusion: _____

_____

_____

_____

_____

Copyright © 1999 Sally Kneidel • *Classroom Critters and the Scientific Method* • Fulcrum Publishing • (800) 992-2908 • www.fulcrum-resources.com

Notes: _____

_____

_____

_____

_____

_____

_____

_____

_____

_____

_____

_____

_____

_____

_____

_____

_____

_____

_____

_____

_____

_____

_____

Index of Experiments

Anoles, 122–136
Color change experiment, 132–136
Food preferences experiment, 122–125
Image response experiment, 126–128
Photograph response experiment, 129–131

Gerbils, 16–21, 32–42, 53–56, 59–68, 73–77
Aggression toward intruders experiment, 53–56
Comparing speeds experiment, 32–36
Confrontation behavior experiment, 64–68
Exploratory behavior experiment, 73–77
Gerbil territories experiment, 59–63
Seeking company experiment, 37–42
Seeking out "correct" turns experiment, 16–21

Goldfish, 94–107, 112–121
Do goldfish hide experiment, 94–97
Effects of Elodea experiment, 105–107
Hand signal training experiment, 119–121
Rate of breathing experiment, 98–101
Rates of movement experiment, 102–104
Seeking company experiment, 112–115
Training goldfish experiment, 116–118

Guppies, 108–115
Hiding place attraction experiment, 108–111
Seeking company experiment, 112–115

Hamsters, 16–21, 32–36, 69–72
Comparing speeds experiment, 32–36
Scent reaction experiment, 69–72
Seeking out "correct" turns experiment, 16–21

Kittens, 137–159
Contact comparisons experiment, 143–147
Contact preference experiment, 137–142
Left- or right-handed experiment, 155–159
Select company experiment, 152–154
Temperature controlled attraction experiment, 148–151

Mice, 1–36, 43–52, 57–58, 78–93
Ability to right themselves experiment, 84–86
Aggression levels of residents and intruders experiment, 57–58
Comparing speed experiment, 32–36
Food reward experiment, 27–31
Forced-turn maze experiment, 22–26
Male "intruders" experiment, 43–47
Odor sensitivity experiment, 78–83
Rope-climbing development experiment, 91–93
Seeking out "correct" turns experiment, 16–21
Sequence of development stages experiment, 87–90
Sex-based intruder experiment, 48–52
Tunnel diameter experiment, 6–10
Tunnel styles experiment, 11–15
Wall-seeker experiment, 1–5

Puppies, 143–147
Contact comparisons experiment, 143–147

EDUCATION RESOURCE CENTER
012 WILLARD HALL
UNIVERSITY OF DELAWARE
NEWARK, DE 19716-2940